Edward de Bono's
Textbook of Wisdom

VIKING

VIKING

Published by the Penguin Group
Penguin Books Ltd, 27 Wrights Lane, London w8 5tz, England
Penguin Books USA Inc., 375 Hudson Street, New York, New York 10014, USA
Penguin Books Australia Ltd, Ringwood, Victoria, Australia
Penguin Books Canada Ltd, 10 Alcorn Avenue, Toronto, Ontario, Canada m4v 3b2
Penguin Books (NZ) Ltd, 182–190 Wairau Road, Auckland 10, New Zealand

Penguin Books Ltd, Registered Offices: Harmondsworth, Middlesex, England

First published 1996
10 9 8 7 6 5 4 3 2 1
First edition

Set in 12/15pt Monotype Baskerville
Typeset by Datix International Limited, Bungay, Suffolk
Printed in England by Clays Ltd, St Ives plc

A CIP catalogue record for this book is available from the British Library

isbn 0–670–87011–0

This is the first edition of The Textbook of Wisdom.

The second edition may be very much better.

But why wait?

I do not know when the second edition will be ready.

Author's Note

There are two parts to the page numbering. The usual numbers and a chapter numbering. So, 6/24 means the sixth page of a section that is twenty-four pages long.

The sections are numbered for ease of reference.

The 'gap' between each section is indicated by a line. If the gap is large the line is longer.

Because the chapters always start on a left-hand page and because diagrams are always on the right-hand page there are sometimes gaps in the text.

 # 1 There is a person at point A. For some reason you want to prevent that person from moving to B. What might you do?

1. You might give no information about B, so that the person is not even aware that B exists.

2. You might give misleading information, so that the person is looking in the wrong direction for B.

3. You might make sure that there is no road between A and B. So there is a 'gap' or the absence of any path.

4. You might build a wall between A and B.

5. You might dig a ditch between A and B. The ditch does not have to be very wide.

6. You might build a wall (or ditch) around B.

7. You might fix a heavy ball and chain to the person's ankle. This would restrict movement in all directions – including moving to B.

You can probably think of a lot more ways of preventing that person getting to B.

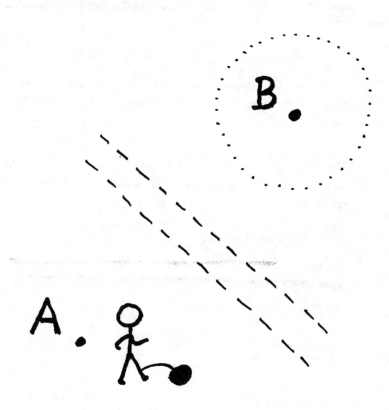

You want to make it as difficult as possible for the person at A to get to B.

 # 2 By far the most effective way of preventing that person getting to B is to provide an easy and attractive path to C.

In all the other ways the person has B firmly in mind and is seeking ways to get there – except where there is no information at all about B. The person might be seeking ways to climb walls, cross ditches and remove the ball and chain.

With the easy and attractive path to C, the person forgets all about B and no longer notices B or the desire to get there.

It is because the mind works this way that 'wisdom' is so important. We do not always want to take the easy and obvious path that our minds and our feelings set out in front of us.

It is the same with 'creativity'. We do not always want to take the easy and obvious traditional path.

By making it very easy and attractive for the person at A to get to C you make it impossible to get to B.

 # 3 Two days ago someone told me that he had come back from an international meeting in Japan. At that meeting there had been an admiral who was very definite, decisive and dogmatic.

Imagine someone walking along the road in the country-side. That person comes to a fork in the road. The person may know the road, may read the road signs, may consult a map, may choose the fork going in the general direction of choice or may choose randomly. What is clear is that the walker has to choose fork C or D. The walker cannot pursue both roads at the same time.

It is possible that the background experience of the dog-matic admiral was the same. You cannot steer a ship in two different directions at the same time. So in steering a ship there is a need to be definite and to make decisions. I have no evidence at all that admirals, in general, are more dogmatic than other people. I am merely putting this forward as an illustrative possibility.

All this is very reasonable. You cannot walk along two roads at the same time and you cannot steer a ship in two different directions at the same time.

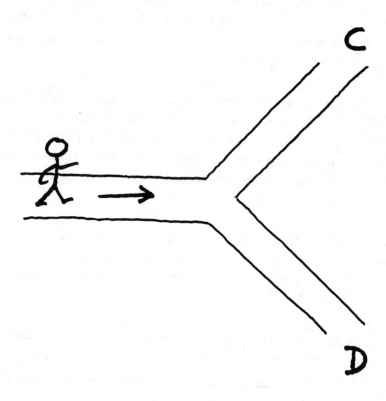

The walker along the road must choose between D and C. It is not possible to walk along both branches at the same time.

 # 4 An investment manager has to consider where to invest the funds that he or she manages. There is no point in putting all the funds into government securities or putting all the funds into the stock market or using all the funds as venture capital.

So the wise investment manager creates a portfolio. Some funds go into government securities. Some funds go into the stock market with blue-chip companies. Some funds are invested in the high-tech sector. Some funds are used for high-risk venture capital. All these things are done at the same time.

Contrast the investment manager with the admiral and the walker. The investment manager can do several different things, in parallel, at the same time. The walker and the admiral could not.

Which is the correct metaphor to keep in our heads to guide our choices, decisions and actions? The answer, of course, is both. It does not have to be one or the other.

Both metaphors have their place. We would not be very wise if we only kept one metaphor in our mind so that all decisions had to be 'one thing' or 'the other'. Nor would it be wise to assume that we could always do all things without making a decision.

It is wisdom which fills your minds with both 'possibilities'. Wisdom is much concerned with the richness of 'possibility'. It is wisdom which helps you decide the metaphor that is most relevant in any particular circumstance. In many cultures you cannot marry more than one

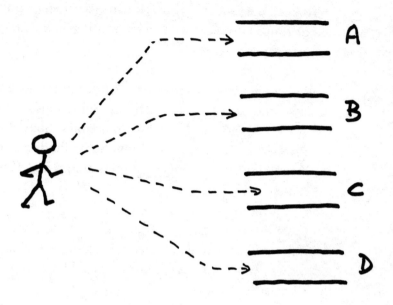

In the portfolio model you can invest in A, B, C and D all at the same time.
Contrast this with the 'road model'.

person at a time. But there is no reason why you should not pursue different and parallel strategies in marketing. All your eggs do not have to be in one basket all the time.

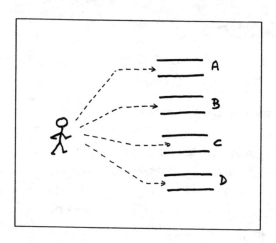

Introduction

 # 5 How dare anyone write a 'textbook' of wisdom?

Surely wisdom is a matter of getting older and 'wiser'? A good claret acquires a mellowness and maturity with age. You cannot accelerate the ageing process in wine. With time, the surface of a new building acquires the patina of age. You cannot fake that artificially.

As you get older you know more. You have experienced more. You have learned more things. You have made more mistakes. You have had more time to talk to other people and to learn from their experiences. More things have happened in your lifetime, both to you and to the world around. You have had longer to reflect on all these things. All this takes time. Perhaps 'wisdom' is simply a generous way of saying that there are some advantages to being old when there seem to be only disadvantages in most areas.

We begin to doubt this simple equating of wisdom with age (and a long white beard) when we find that some older people are not wise at all and some younger people are 'wise beyond their years'.

Do you have to wait until you get old before you can become wise? Surely there are some general principles,

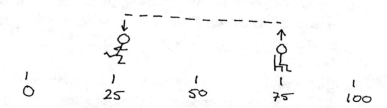

You do not have to have lived a long time to benefit from the experience of those who have.

guidelines and even 'thinking tools' that could help us to be wiser? We do not have to learn everything through personal experience. We can also seek to benefit from the experience of others. That is what education is supposed to be about.

Obviously, I do believe that there are enough useful things that can be learned about wisdom to fill a very short 'textbook' of wisdom. These are not all new things. They do not have to be. Engineers use wheels all the time. But the wheel was invented a long time ago.

Will reading this book make the reader wiser? It could. I hope it will. But reading a cookery book does not turn you into an instant gourmet chef. You need to show interest in what you are reading and also you need to practise. Then you might become a good cook. Some talent is also useful.

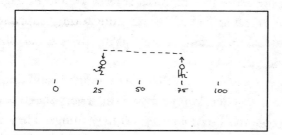

 # 6 Wisdom is not at all the same as cleverness. I have known many people who are very clever indeed within their own fields (even winning Nobel prizes) but not especially 'wise' outside their own fields of study. Cleverness is like a lens with a very sharp focus. Wisdom is more like a wide-angle lens.

In the same way, wisdom is not a function of intelligence. Many people whose education has been simple are much wiser than those who have learned a lot from books. The explanation is that 'living' may teach more about wisdom than traditional books (apart from this one).

Wisdom is more about perspective than about detail. Cleverness is about how we get information and how we use information. Wisdom is about how the information fits into the world around and our own values.

Cleverness is like knowing, technically, how to cook a superb meal. Wisdom is like designing a meal to fit the available ingredients and also to fit what we feel like eating at this moment.

Cleverness is like having a library full of books. Wisdom is knowing which book to read at this moment.

Wisdom is the art with which perception crafts experience to serve our values.

A potter crafts the clay to create a pot that both serves a practical function and also pleases us aesthetically. This goes beyond mere technical skill, as Socrates would have appreciated, with his distinction between 'technique' and 'virtue'.

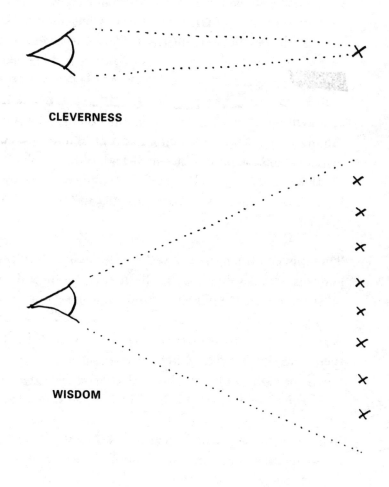

CLEVERNESS

WISDOM

Cleverness is a narrow focus even if it is very sharp. Wisdom is a wide-angle focus which takes in much more.

 # 7 I have often said, and written, that humour is by far the most significant behaviour of the human brain. In information terms, reason is a relatively cheap commodity obtained by running any sorting system backwards.

Humour is significant for two reasons. The first reason is that humour indicates a special type of information system in the brain. Humour tells us, in broad terms, how the brain works. Humour indicates a self-organizing information system. This is not unlike the way rainfall on a landscape organizes itself into streams and rivers and valleys. In a similar way, information organizes itself into patterns.

There are the main patterns. Then there might be side patterns. Activity flows along the main pattern and the other patterns are suppressed. So the flow goes from A to B. You cannot go from A to C. But you can easily go from C to A. Creativity involves 'somehow' getting to C and then, suddenly, seeing the path to A. The tools of lateral thinking help you move 'laterally' from the main track to C. Provocation is of great help. (I shall explain later.)

In humour the situation or the teller of the story leads you along the main track and then, suddenly, takes you to C. Once there you see the 'connection' and, possibly, laugh.

The second reason that humour is so important is that humour takes place in 'perception'. Outside technical matters, perception is the most important part of thinking. Traditional education may not have given you this impression. Most of the faults of thinking are faults of perception.

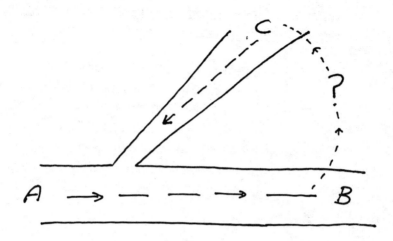

There is the main track set up by our sequence of experience. We go along this. We cannot get access to the side track. But if, somehow, we jump or move laterally to the side track then in hindsight it makes sense. The route from A to C is roundabout but from C to A is direct. This is the basis of both humour and creativity. Creative ideas are usually logical and even obvious in hindsight.

Wisdom takes place in the 'perception' area. Wisdom is about broader perception, deeper perception, richer perception, etc. If you have a good sense of humour you have the potential to be wise.

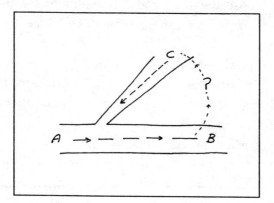

 # 8   The format of this book is a little bit unusual. There are no headings and subheadings and sub-subheadings. There are notes and paragraphs. Sometimes the jump between one paragraph and another may be large.

There is no need to read the book from cover to cover. You can dip into the book and read a paragraph at a time. You can go back and read parts again. The intention is that the overlay of the different points and examples will gradually form a coherent picture. This is more like the way we learn from life itself. Things are not laid out neatly in boxes. We come across the same things from different angles. We taste the same fruit on different occasions. Gradually we build up our understanding of the world around us. This is the way I run my seminars. Sometimes participants feel insecure without a detailed road map. They need to know exactly where they are going next. They need to know where they have just been. I tell them that it will unfold as we go along. There is a plan. It is not a matter of rambling or drifting. As the driver of the 'coach', I have the plan and the road map. Relax and enjoy the scenery.

 # 9   Some of the matters in this book may have been touched upon in previous books of mine. There are fundamentals of mathematics which do not change or go in and out of fashion. There are a limited number of musical notes and it is through combinations of these basic notes that music is composed.

Since so much of my work is in the field of thinking, perception and creativity, it is hardly surprising that these are the basic elements of 'wisdom'. In a sense, I have always been writing about wisdom indirectly. I am now writing about wisdom directly.

 # 10 This is not a 'textbook' on how to run your life, even though a reader may at times interpret it in that way. It is intended to be a textbook of 'wisdom'. If you set out to become a little wiser it is possible that you may run your life in a better way. If you put better fuel in your car you may get a better performance.

This book is not intended to give you ready-made answers to problems, difficulties and confusions. The book is about 'wisdom' which may help you find a way out, if there is one, or help you to adjust if there is not.

 # 11 Those who are ready to be outraged that anyone should have the cheek to write a book about wisdom will be even more outraged to learn that this book was written in four mornings between 16 August and 20 August 1995 at Palazzo Marnisi in Malta. It was too hot to write in the afternoons.

Why should I reveal this fact? The effect is likely to be negative. When philosophers spend their whole lives writing a book about wisdom, how dare someone set out to write a book about wisdom in four days? That people should be outraged has never much worried me. Some people like to be outraged. It makes them feel significant.

Writing a book in a short time allows a natural flow of the thoughts and material. If you painstakingly refine and re-refine every point you may make fewer mistakes and reveal deeper intricacies – but the book is likely to be much less readable.

I much prefer the reader to take the different points that I put forward and to reflect upon them and to elaborate upon them in his or her mind. In that way the different points can be enriched. There is not much point in disagreeing with me unless you have an alternative point of view which you prefer. If the book stimulates you to form this point of view, I accept that it may be better than mine, worse than mine or a reasonable alternative to my point of view.

I try to avoid terms like 'must' and 'cannot', 'never' and 'always' but am not 'always' successful in doing so. Such terms invite nit-picking disagreement where someone will point out some very special set of circumstances where something does not apply – even if it does apply in 99 per cent of cases. Socrates was in the habit of doing just this. For my purposes, terms like 'by and large' or 'usually' are practical and useful.

The emphasis has to be on 'usefulness'. That is exactly why it is called a 'textbook' of wisdom.

Perception

 # 12   'What is the definition of "wisdom"?'

'Wisdom is that quality which "wise" people show.'

'What is the definition of "wise people"?'

'People who show "wisdom".'

That may seem a rather stupid exchange, but it is not. Definitions have their place in law, philosophy, science, medicine and various other specific areas. When you go to the supermarket to buy 'low-fat' food you would really like to know exactly what is meant by 'low-fat'.

In many other areas definitions have no practical value and are really a game with words. The definition of wisdom is always likely to appear unsatisfactory.

'How do you perceive wisdom?'

'I see older people who do not jump to conclusions. They take a broader view. They give very practical answers. They take a balanced view. They are not so dogmatic. They are more tolerant. They look deeper into things. They can generate and consider alternatives. They look at things differently and from many angles.'

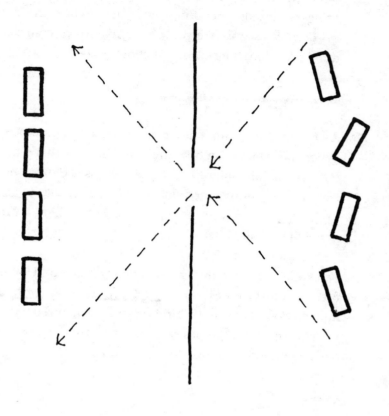

Perception is how the mind organizes the information that is coming in from the world outside.

This is a complex perception made up of a bundle of different images, qualities, behaviours, etc. Perception brings a bundle of things together. When the word 'wisdom' is used we trigger that bundle which comes into mind both consciously and subconsciously.

 # 13 A person born with thick corneal opacities cannot see. When, later in life, an operation gives sight to that person, the person still cannot see. Everything is a blur of light, colours and disorganized shapes. The person has to learn to 'organize' this information in the brain. That is what perception is all about.

Perception is not only what is physically in front of our eyes (or other senses) but what the brain does with this information. How is the information structured? What information from the past is brought up to integrate with the present information?

 # 14 We live in the world we 'see'. But the world we see is not the physical world around us but the 'perceived' world in our minds. The physical world may be exactly the same but different people will see different things.

A holiday is half gone. Or, half the holiday is still to come.

A glass is half empty. Or, the glass is half full.

The mistake is a disaster. Or, the mistake teaches a useful lesson.

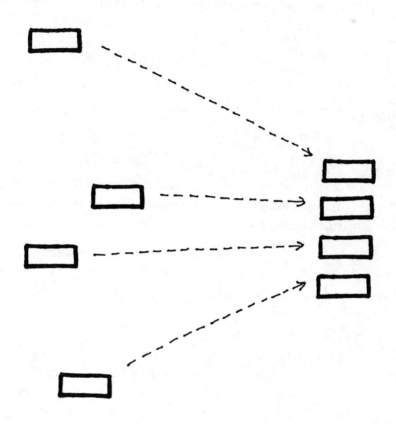

Perception provides the ingredients for processing, as in mathematics, logic, etc.

A plate of chicken is placed on the table before a person. How does that person perceive the food?

1. A vegetarian does not want to eat the chicken but is timid about asking for something else.

2. A hungry person looks with delight and anticipation at the food.

3. A person who is trying to lose weight wonders how many calories there are in the chicken and remembers the fat is mainly in the skin.

4. A person who has a stomach upset is nauseated by the smell of the food.

5. A person who has just read about an outbreak of salmonella infection is suspicious and cautious. Would it be risky to eat the chicken?

For each person the physical appearance of the chicken is exactly the same as would be shown if each person took a photograph from the same angle. But the mind does not take photographs. The mind brings in information, experience, frames, present contexts, feelings and emotions. All these get organized by perception to give us 'the way we look at the situation'.

 # 15 We can caricature the three intellectual ages of man as follows:

0 to 5 years is the age of 'why?'.

Children are continuously asking 'why', not so much to seek explanations but just to get more information and to link up their small pieces of perceived world into a bigger perception.

5 to 12 years is the age of 'why not'.

Here youngsters have a great deal of intellectual energy and enterprise. They are probing for information. They can play with ideas. They are free to be creative and to try out new possibilities.

12 to 75+ years is the age of 'because'.

We are now so tethered by considerations that the world has to be the way it is because any change is not acceptable or is too disturbing.

Over time our individual perceptions settle down to give us our personal view of the world. That is how we see the world. That is the world in which we live and act. That world may be full of inadequacies, prejudices, stereotypes and confusions. That is the only world we have.

 # 16 Most of the faults of thinking are faults of perception. Faults of logic outside of special 'teaser puzzles' are actually quite rare. You can usually tie someone up in logical knots with a carefully prepared conundrum, but in ordinary life people are quite logical. For a very long time now I have been pointing out that perception is the key part of thinking. David Perkins of Harvard University told me

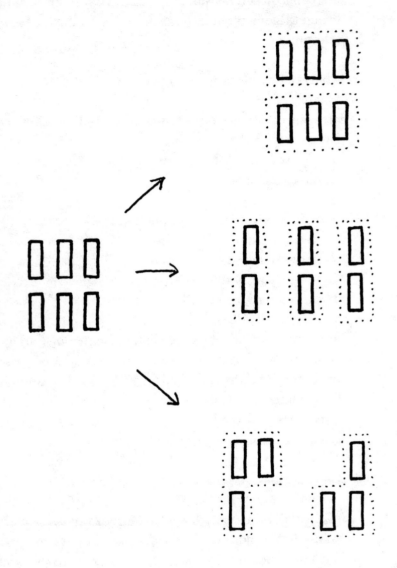

We can look at exactly the same thing and yet divide it up in many different ways. Perception decides how we structure the world around us.

that his research showed that most of the faults in thinking are faults of perception: seeing only part of the situation, bringing along an inadequate frame and using emotional selection of information, etc.

Many of the deficiencies in behaviour could also be seen as faults of perception (at least in part):
arrogance, selfishness, despair, overreaction and dependence, etc.

 # 17 A man is offered a job in another town. The pay and prospects are much better. There are good schools for the children. Whenever he raises the subject his wife gets very distressed and upset. He is telling his friend about this. The friend suggests that it is a matter of 'emotional blackmail'. Suddenly the man has the 'possibility' of looking at the situation differently. It does not mean that this is indeed a case of emotional blackmail, or that emotional blackmail even exists. But a new possible perception has been offered.

 # 18 As languages get more developed they acquire a great flexibility of expression. This means that an arrangement of existing words can be used to describe almost anything. As this 'descriptive' capacity of language grows, so there is less need for 'perception' words which only describe one particular thing. Why have lots of 'perception' words when an arrangement of ordinary words can describe anything?

The Inuit in Canada (or at least some groups) are said to have twenty words between 'like' and 'dislike' – perhaps because at one time they were all huddled closely together in an igloo for months on end. There is said to be one word for:
'I like you very much but I would not want to go seal hunting with you.'

It would be nice to have a word which by itself indicated all the following:
'It is not your fault and I still like you very much but right now I am feeling very edgy and you are indeed irritating me.'

We could also have a 'perception' word for:
'I know you have to say the things you are saying. I do not believe them and you do not believe them. You do not even believe that I believe them. We both know it is a routine which has to be performed.'

The Japanese seem much better at subtle 'perception' words which embrace special situations.

---

19 I introduced the concept of the 'logic bubble' in a previous book of mine (*Future Positive*, Penguin 1990). This is a 'perception' phrase. What it signifies is that we should assume – even if it is not true – that everyone is behaving logically within his or her 'bubble' of perception. This means: the way that person perceives the situation and the values that person perceives to be involved in the situation. So, instead of mentally accusing that person of being stupid or malicious, one acknowledges that person's

logical behaviour and seeks to understand the perceptual 'bubble' within which it is so logical.

It is very much part of wisdom to consider such 'logic bubbles'.

────────────

 # 20 Have you ever seen a concept walking down the street – or anywhere at any time of day or night? Concepts only live in the mind and are created solely by our willingness to create concepts. What is the concept of a car steering-wheel? 'A method for allowing the hands to control the direction of the front wheel for steering purposes.' Once we have extracted the concept we can find other, alternative ways of carrying out that concept. That is why concepts are a very key part of human thinking.

Concepts are part of perception. We have to perceive the concepts. You do someone a favour. It could be out of generosity or it could be that you want that person 'to owe you one'. That is exploiting the concept of 'obligation'.

Concepts can tie together a bundle of things: 'I want a concept for rewarding motorists who could choose to drive into the city but prefer to keep their cars at home.' Concepts can extract the 'essence' or function of something: 'The key concept of democracy is to give people the illusion that they choose their government.'

Wisdom can build up a repertoire of concepts which are not obvious and not available to everyone. Concepts of 'value' are extremely important. You may worry if another restaurant opens too close to you. Then you console yourself with the thought that if the street becomes a 'restaurant area' you may end up getting more business than before.

 # 21 How good is perception? Is human perception adequate for our needs? The unfortunate answer is that human perception is becoming increasingly inadequate for our needs. When we are dealing with complex interactive systems human perception simply cannot cope. The outcome of such situations is often counter-intuitive and we cannot guess or get a feel for it. For such situations we may need such techniques as the flowscape technique of water logic (see *Water Logic*, Penguin 1994) or interactive models on computers. We shall need wisdom to set up such models so that they include all the relevant factors. We also need to be wise enough to know the limitations of human perception.

 # 22 Age can provide richer experience, but not necessarily so. Professor John Edwards is fond of saying that a teacher with twenty years' experience may indeed have twenty years' experience or may have twenty times a one-year experience. If you always look at things in the same way then more experience only provides more books on the same shelf.

Age permits you to have more experience but only if you permit yourself to be open to new experiences. If you never change your mind, why have one? Have a sign on

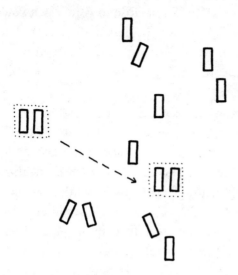

We can look at the world through a chosen 'frame'. This sensitizes our attention, so we notice what we set out to notice.

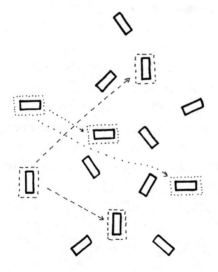

We can deliberately direct attention so that we pick out what we want. There are attention-directing thinking tools.

your desk which says: 'Same thinking as yesterday, last year or ten years ago.'

 # 23 You are in a plane that is coming in to land at Heathrow airport in London. The plane passes over several car parks. You say to yourself: 'I am going to notice all the cars coloured red.' You look at the car park and all the cars coloured red jump out at you. Red is a fairly common colour. So you choose 'bright blue'. This colour is much more rare and your eye scans over the cars. Suddenly a bright blue car jumps out of the mass.

There are two important points about this simple experiment. The first point is that you are giving instructions to your own brain. The second is that you are 'sensitizing' the brain to certain types of input.

A suspicious wife notices that when her husband comes home late in the evening his tie is a different length from when he left in the morning. Her suspicious mind immediately jumps to the conclusion that perhaps he has a mistress. The emotion of jealousy has sensitized perception in the same way as the attention-directing instruction. In fact the poor fellow has just played a game of squash.

 # 24 Why is 'thinking' important? Because without thinking we can only act in the following ways:

1. Act purely on instinct like insects.

2. Repeat the usual routines.

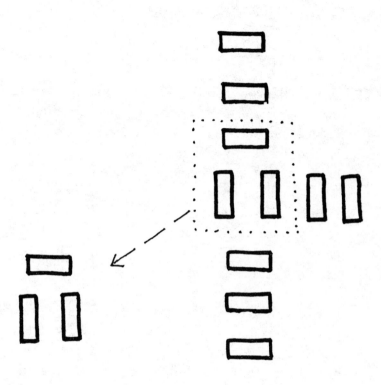

One of the major faults of perception is picking out just one part of the situation and ignoring the rest.

3. Do what someone else decides and orders.

4. Follow the emotion of the moment.

 # 25 Part of thinking consists of giving ourselves 'attention-directing' instructions. Just as we could direct our brain to 'pick out blue cars', so we can also direct our brain to look in different directions. The attention-directing tools of the CoRT programme (for schools) or the DATT programme (for business) do exactly this. The first lesson in the CoRT programme is called the PMI and it is an attention-directing instruction which asks the thinker to look first at the 'Plus' points, then at the 'Minus' points and finally at the 'Interesting' points.

In Korea, where I had been chairing a meeting of Nobel prizewinners from around the world, I was asked to teach 'thinking' at the local primary school. It had to be done through an interpreter. I drew a figure with a third arm emerging from the chest. I then asked the students to do a PMI. Some of the results were as follows:

Plus points:

– spare arm in case of injury

– you could hold on to the ladder and use both hands for the tools

– you could hold someone and punch them with both fists.

Minus points:

– you could not sleep on your face

– you might have to cut a hole in your clothes

– when you got old and had arthritis, you would have another place to have arthritis.

Interesting points:

– would you be 'centre'-handed instead of right-handed?

– on which side would the thumb be?

– the rules for sports might have to change.

Later on I asked the same youngsters to 'do a PMI on doing the PMI'. One nine-year-old girl said that if everyone did a PMI then no one would ever get married.

There is a whole range of such attention-directing tools (consequences, values, priorities, other people's views, etc.) For information contact the CoRT Thinking Programme:

UK	*International*
Svend Holst	APTT
European Head Office	10520 New York Avenue
Prospect House	Des Moines
Great Missenden	Iowa 50322
Bucks. HP16 0BG	USA

In a way these simple tools are 'wisdom' tools because they increase the breadth of perception.

26 What is a pattern, a road, a track or a path? The functional definition is very simple.

'If the change of state from the present state takes place in a strongly preferred direction then you are in a pattern, on a road, along a track, etc.'

In all these cases when you are on a road the chances of you moving along the road are much greater than of your jumping off that road.

As a self-organizing information system (see *Mechanism of Mind*, Penguin 1990; *I am Right – You are Wrong*, Penguin 1991) the brain sets up patterns. These are flows of activity from one area to another. At any one moment the flow is much more likely to go towards one defined (and pre-sensitized area) than to another.

It is the very excellence of the mind to form such patterns. Without them we should not be able to get up in the morning, get to work, recognize our friends, read, write or do any work at all. We should be much admiring of and grateful for this wonderful capacity of the brain to form routine patterns. That is the basis of perception.

27 You find some money in an envelope lying on the ground. You pick it up. Why should you not keep it? That pattern is sensible and attractive. Then your mind, your conscience or your thinking introduces a super-pattern: 'What is the "honest" thing to do?' This super-pattern wins and you take the envelope along to the police station.

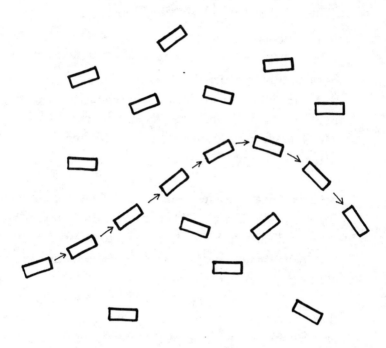

We are on a road, track or pattern when the next step in any one direction is much easier than a step in any other direction.

There are all sorts of super-patterns:

'I shall do what God wants me to do.'

'I must do what is right.'

Sometimes a politician gets such a strong sense of style that the politician no longer considers the situation in itself but uses the following super-pattern: 'What would Mrs Thatcher do in this situation?' And then she does just that.

Someone once told me a story of how he was trapped in a car park late at night. Then he said to himself: 'What would Edward de Bono do in this situation?' Apparently that helped him find a way out through the car park entrance rather than the exit.

It has always been the aim of religion, of education and of family upbringing to suggest such super-patterns to guide perception and thence behaviour.

In the absence of such formal super-patterns there is a tendency to fall back on the most available super-pattern: what is everyone else doing? What is the gang doing? What is the peer group view of this?

 # 28 Once it has been thought, a thought cannot be un-thought. Once a perceptual possibility has been suggested it cannot be cancelled. You can let that pattern atrophy. You can have that pattern lead to a negative. You can try to put it alongside another pattern.

An overweight man has a plate of food in front of him. He tries various super-patterns:

– he is dieting

– his doctor has frightened him with tales of problems caused by overweight

– he imagines his coronary arteries clogging up.

These competing patterns might work. One useful approach is to set up a positive pattern:

– he takes pride in the 'achievement' of leaving a lot of the food on the plate.

 # 29 Wisdom is to do with the broader view. Wisdom is to do with the deeper view. Wisdom is to do with the richer view. Wisdom seeks to take the 'helicopter view', so that everything can be seen in perspective and in relation to everything else.

Wisdom insists that you think slowly, very slowly. If you think fast you are very likely to be trapped by the habitual pattern.

As you get older everyone around seems to get younger. Grown adults seem to be acting with the innocence and simplicity of children. We do not fear children because they are innocent and transparent. So we get to treat adults in the same way. There are also some 'child monsters' who are selfish and demanding. Wisdom is the ability to see through surface appearances.

Wisdom is the ability to imagine possibilities and to consider them. Wisdom is the disinclination to get trapped in the easy judgements of false certainties.

 # 30 Wisdom takes place in perception. Othello moved too surely from the 'possibility' of Desdemona's infidelity to a fatal certainty. That was a marked lack of wisdom due to perceptions driven by strong emotion.

Throughout this textbook of wisdom the emphasis will be on perception. Emotions are largely unaffected by logic. Perception triggers emotions and perception can change emotions.

One boy in a carpentry class in an institute for young offenders was about to attack one of the officers with a hammer. He then thought back to his CoRT thinking lesson about 'consequences', gave a shrug and put the hammer down.

 # 31 What about changing the world? It was George Bernard Shaw who said that progress was always due to the unreasonable man. The reasonable man adapted to the existing situation. It was the unreasonable man who sought to change the situation.

1. You can seek to change the world (the basis of Western progress).

2. You can seek to change yourself (Buddhist and Eastern approach).

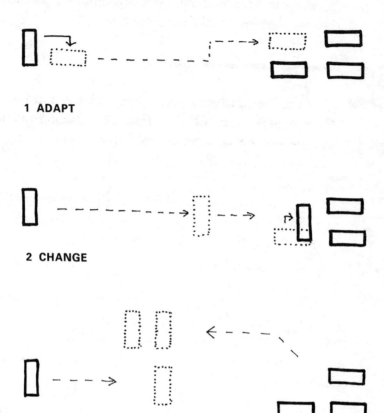

1 ADAPT

2 CHANGE

3 PERCEIVE

1. You can seek to adapt to the world as it is.
2. You can seek to change the world.
3. You can seek to change your perception of the world.

3. You can seek to change your perceptions, and also to change the world as a result.

 # 32 'Yonder Park' is where possibilities and the future happen. Perception is our mind wandering in that park. Wisdom is our observation as we wander.

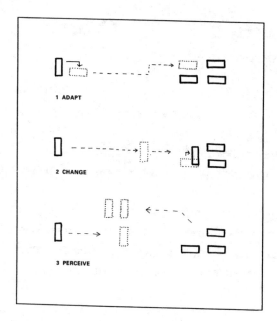

Now and   Then

'The Edge Effect'

 # 33   One of the prime duties that wisdom is called upon to perform is to cope with the problem of 'now' and 'then'.

The youngster drops out of school to earn good money and to have a less boring time. That is 'now'. Later the earning capacity of that youngster is substantially below that of his classmates who got more education.

You meet and get swept off your feet by this charming Romeo with dashing looks, more confidence than anyone you have ever met and a fast sports car. Later he is a boring, lazy, womanizing slob.

The bull cannot leave the field because there is a thin string-like wire and if he touches the wire he gets a sharp electric shock. He stays well away from the wire.

There is no fence around the house but the dog does not stray. She knows that if she approaches the boundary then the little box she carries gives her a sharp shock.

A woman in a bad marriage has decided to get out but cannot face the moment of telling the bad-tempered husband.

_____

 # 34 The 'edge effect' works both ways. There is something marvellous that you want to do but you cannot do it because the very first step is so very difficult. Your future career depends on your phoning someone – but you are too shy to phone.

The other way round, there is something which is immediately enticing but the long-term effect is bad. You smoke your first cigarette because it makes you feel grown up and 'one of the gang'. Later in life when you are trying so hard to give up, you wish you had never started.

A journey of a thousand miles starts with one pace. If you are unable to take that pace the rest is unimportant.

The pull of an immediate temptation is strong, as any reformed alcoholic knows.

Medicine tastes very bad. It is truly horrid, just as an injection is truly painful. So why do children take the medicine?

– because they are bullied into taking it
– because mummy might not love them if they do not
– because they believe the medicine will make them better.

People suffer considerable agonies at the dentist because:

– it seems necessary
– to look more beautiful
– to prevent future toothache
– to prevent future tooth loss.

EDGE EFFECT: NEGATIVE

EDGE EFFECT: POSITIVE

In the 'negative' edge effect you do not take the next step because it is difficult.

In the 'positive' edge effect you take the next step because it is very easy to take.

35   Religion has been remarkably successful in controlling immediate action and resistance to temptation through offering very long-term benefits: you roast in hell or felicitate in heaven.

In Canada, and possibly some other countries, the death rate from lung cancer in women through smoking is now higher than that of breast cancer. If you were to ask women they would choose to remove the threat of breast cancer through an act of their own choice, I suspect most women would claim that indeed they would exert that choice. But smoking is a choice and they do not choose to make that choice.

It is therefore surprising that in Christianity the very long-term threat of hell or promise of heaven should be able to affect immediate action. But religion also acts through much more immediate mechanisms.

There is inner guilt and conscience. There is the fear that God will not love you any more. There is the condemnation of peer pressure, since your peers may be watching to see how you behave. There is the powerful mechanism of ritual. If you omit the ritual this is like a spiritual insult. Your lack of faith is immediately made tangible and visible to yourself and to others.

The most powerful effect of religion is to provide those super-patterns which compete with the 'immediate patterns'. Such super-patterns prevent us succumbing to 'temptation'. Such super-patterns persuade people to make the ultimate sacrifice of their lives for their beliefs. Faith is the most powerful of super-patterns.

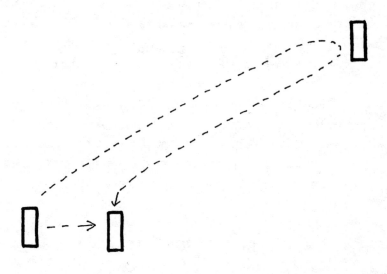

Religion deals with very long term consequences, but these are made immediate through guilt or peer pressure.

 # 36 Capitalism is another successful device for preferring long-term consequences over short-term gain. You could spend the money and enjoy it. Or, you could invest it in a machine which will earn income for you in the future.

There are 162,000 students (1995) in the University of California; 40 per cent of these students are of Asian origin. Yet there is only 5.5 per cent of Asians in the population. So 5.5 per cent of the population is providing 40 per cent of the university students. The explanation is that 'education' is part of the investment culture of Asians. You invest time, effort and family discipline in education. That is an expectation and not a matter of choice.

In ethnic conflicts, as in the former Yugoslavia, you hear of atrocities against your group. So you seek the protection of your local warlord. Tit-for-tat atrocities are carried out. All sides long for peace but at every moment they have to take action which makes that peace impossible. There is a need somehow to break the continuity of the local fighting.

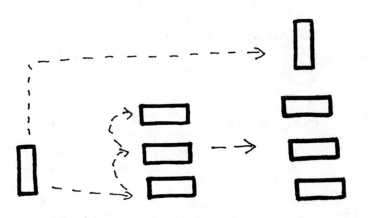

CONSUMPTION

CAPITALISM

Capitalism means forgoing immediate consumption in order to invest for long-term benefits.

 # 37 It could be imagined that the biological purpose of anger and aggression might be to drive us through the edge effect. There is something that needs to be done but you do not like doing it. Anger drives you to do it. Anger might replace the fear that otherwise held you back. So you work yourself up into a 'state' in order to cross the 'barrier'.

Conversely, fear acts as an edge effect. Fear of taking the first step keeps us within boundaries. Fear of the electric shock keeps the bull within the electric fence. A stern tone of voice from father keeps the child from misbehaving. Signals are often enough.

It is ironic that a human smile is a remnant of the aggressive baring of teeth in animals. One animal bares its teeth to indicate that another animal is in danger of being attacked. Perhaps the connection is that a smile means: 'I am relating to you.' The 'relating' is more important than the quality of the relationship.

 # 38 Dealing with the edge effect is very much part of wisdom. So we might summarize some of the different approaches.

The Culture Approach

Certain behaviour becomes so much part of the culture (general, or within an organization or family) that you are not even aware of the edge effect. The example of Asian students studying hard applies here.

The Awareness Approach

This is almost the opposite of the culture approach. In the awareness approach you 'identify' the edge effect. You make it very clear to yourself perceptually. Once you know what you are dealing with it may become easier to cross some 'ditch' or to avoid some immediate temptation. You say to yourself: 'This is an edge-effect situation.'

The Consequences Approach

You spell out the consequences. You direct your attention to the consequences. The hope is that an awareness of the consequences will guide you over the edge effect. If you know how harmful smoking might be then you do not smoke. If you know how dangerous drugs are then you do not start. In practice, the consequences effect is much weaker than it should be. You always believe that the bad consequences 'will happen only to other people'.

Immediate Consequences

How can those remote consequences be made more immediate? For religion, ritual, guilt, peer pressure all serve this purpose. The approval or disapproval of someone close by can help. There is a design task: how can we make the remote consequences more immediate? If your skin turned yellow very soon after you took drugs then you would not take them. Fashion and peer pressure are powerful but can go either way. Fashion and peer pressure can get you to do things you ought to do but also to do things that are not helpful.

Super-patterns

These are the overriding patterns of self-image, religious principles, conscience, etc. If they are strong and well cared for they can work very effectively. The difficulty is that the other pattern still exerts its attraction. It is like a reformed alcoholic still having the tempting drink in front of him and reminding himself, 'I am a reformed alcoholic.'

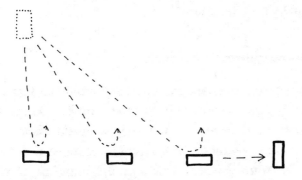

Looking ahead to the consequences. If you push against the tower it will collapse.

A super-pattern is an overriding model which permanently seeks to alter behaviour.

Alternative Pattern

This again is a design task. Can we design another pattern which takes over? The dieter who chooses to get a sense of achievement by seeing how much food she can leave on the plate is now working towards achievement.

The Emotion Approach

As suggested earlier, anger can get you to do things you do not want to do and fear can stop you doing things you do want to do. The trouble is that it is rather difficult to switch such emotions on and off as required.

The Small-step Approach

If there is a difficult letter that you do not want to write then you tell yourself you are only writing a 'draft' version. When you have written the draft you find it serves your purpose very well. So you send it. Real-estate agents sometimes want you to pay a small token deposit. You do not want to lose this so you move on to the next stage and eventually buy the house.

Changing-context Approach

If you change the context completely then the fear and inertia that have held you back can disappear. So if there is something that you know you have to do but cannot get around to doing then changing the context is a useful first step. You might go away on holiday and make your decision somewhere else.

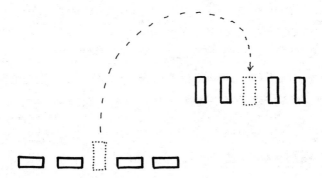

If you change the context then things fit in more easily.

 # 39 It could be said that reconciling the immediate situation with the longer-term view is the essence of civilization.

———

 # 40 There are people who want to live only for today and have fun today. Tomorrow will be coped with when tomorrow arrives. If you are fit, healthy and have confidence in yourself then you will adjust to whatever circumstance arises. This is an attractive philosophy provided 'getting by' and 'having fun' are sufficient. They may well be for the moment. But will they be later? Young hippies and very old hippies are attractive, but it is not so much fun in between.

Then there are those who are forever 'working for the future'. For such people there is never a 'now' or 'today'. If they reach one stage then they must work towards the next. If the enjoyment of work is a high value, this makes sense. But if work is a means to an end, one has to ask when that 'end' is going to be reached.

Achievement is a value just as much as enjoyment. There are personal choices as to how the two get mixed.

As always, wisdom is about balance.

Some people live for today and some only for a future which never arrives as it is always ahead.

Truth, Certainty and Arrogance

 # 41 By the age of twenty-six Alexander the Great had conquered the whole known world. He had even gone as far as India. What was the explanation behind this astonishing feat? The first explanation is that he was an extremely able and gifted person. The second explanation is that the great Aristotle was his tutor. So Aristotle taught him reason, logic and wisdom, and these qualities contributed to his success. The third explanation is that Aristotle, using his 'box' logic, gave Alexander immense confidence in his decisions. It was this decisiveness which then led him to success. It may have been a mixture of all three explanations and of others not suggested here (like very able lieutenants).

Confidence and certainty make for strong decisions and leadership. The confidence of the Normans swept them into England and as far south as Malta in the Mediterranean. The confidence of the Romans and the British created their respective empires.

When does confidence become arrogance? Is your 'confidence' when viewed by someone else no more than 'arrogance'?

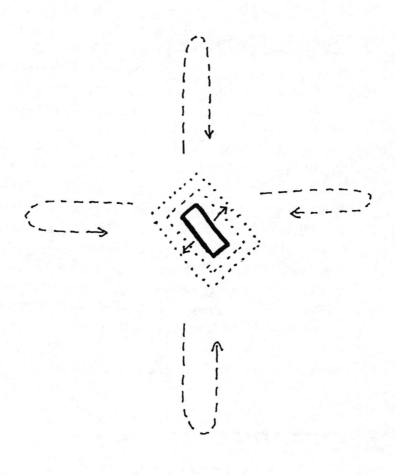

Confidence is a matter of opening up to the world around. Arrogance believes in the sufficiency of an internal world.

The dividing line between confidence and arrogance is very fine but the difference is great. If you think that statement is contradictory, consider two cars going fast along a road in opposite directions. They are close together for a moment but very different in their performance. Arrogance is a shutting off of input. Arrogance is isolating. Arrogance means you do not want and do not need to listen to anyone else. Arrogance is the ultimate 'system' sin. The human system is thereby detached from the world around.

Confidence is just as decisive as arrogance in its performance. But confidence allows input and seeks out input. If you are truly confident, you do not mind listening to other opinions and considering alternatives. You are confident you will do the best. You may even be confident that your opinions will not change and therefore do not mind exposing them to discussion.

Arrogance is almost the exact opposite of wisdom. Confidence is the basis of wisdom.

#**42** From the earliest age we crave certainty in an uncertain world. A baby probably likes to know that if he or she cries in a certain way then mother will appear to feed him or her. We like to know where we are and what we are doing.

An animal likes to be able to recognize, with confidence, its food, its enemies and its potential mates. That is how the world goes round.

An animal cannot afford to have a philosophical discus-

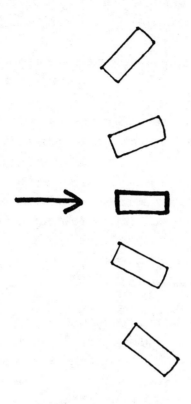

Our brains like certainty. We like certainty. We hate vagueness, instability and uncertainty.

sion on the nature of a berry every time it wants to eat a berry. Much better to recognize the berry instantly, and to get on and eat it.

So the search for recognition and certainty is very useful and very powerful.

The brain is designed exactly to serve this purpose. The brain sets up 'patterns' based on its experience. When something falls within the 'catchment area' of that pattern then the brain recognizes that thing at once. So the brain works very well to put together things that are similar and to separate things that are different (see *I am Right – You are Wrong*, Penguin 1991).

 # 43   A child with a rash is taken by its father to the doctor. The doctor looks at the rash and immediately thinks of a number of possible 'boxes'. The rash could be an allergy. The rash may be no more than sunburn. The rash could be measles. So the doctor looks for some more evidence that will help her decide into which 'box' to place the condition. The doctor carries out a closer examination and asks some questions. When the doctor is satisfied that the diagnosis is 'measles' then the doctor knows exactly how to treat the child. The measles box is standard and the treatment is also standard.

The cluster of features that make up the term 'measles' (the label on that box) have been established by years of experience. The course of the measles illness is also well known through years of experience. The treatment of measles has been established by medical research and is, hopefully, up to date.

So the system is very simple and very effective. You have the standard measles box. You see whether the patient has the features which place the patient's condition in that 'box'. Then the label on the box also tells you the standard way of treating measles.

So the 'box' is a powerful way of connecting up years of experience with the way to treat a particular child.

This is the way the brain itself works when it forms 'patterns'. This is also the way Aristotle formalized our thinking system.

———

 # 44 The Greek Gang of Three formalized the thinking habits that we use to this day. Socrates was concerned with argument and with removing 'untruth'. He felt that if you removed all 'untruth' through critical attack, then you must be left with the 'truth'.

Plato was concerned with the 'inner truth' within things and with the search for that truth. He was influenced by Pythagoras, who had shown that there were ultimate inner truths in mathematics.

Aristotle put everything together as an operating system. There were categories and definitions that were set up by experience and clarified by argument. When you came across something, you 'judged' in which box that something belonged. Then you knew exactly what to do about it, just as the doctor knew what to do about measles. If the matter was complex then you sought to 'analyse' it down into smaller parts that were easier to recognize. The assumption is that every complex thing is made up of standard parts, just as all music is a combination of the basic notes.

Does this system work? It works very well indeed. It is practical, effective and simple. It provides the certainty we need.

But what if the boxes are old-fashioned? What if the judgement is biased? The system still works very well but the results can be dangerous.

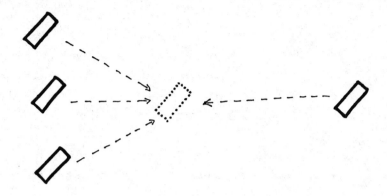

From experience we form boxes and definitions. Then we judge into which standard box a new experience fits.

 # 45 How many people actually want to live at the North Pole? I suspect that very few people actually want to live on a sheet of ice in the cold. But how many people use 'north' as a direction for navigating a boat, flying an airliner, hiking through the country, setting directions on a map or architect's plan, etc.? Obviously, 'north' is much more useful as a 'direction' than as a 'destination'.

It is somewhat the same with 'truth'. We want the truth. We try to find the truth. We do science to find the truth. Truth is a wonderful direction in which to be heading.

Truth as a 'destination' gives us values and certainty. It can also give us arrogance and persecution: 'I have the truth, therefore everyone else must be wrong.' This may indeed be 'true'. It can happen that one person is right and everyone else is wrong.

When a doctor in the 1940s suggested that stomach ulcers were caused by an infection, everyone laughed at him. Today's evidence suggests that he was right after all and everyone else was wrong.

———

There is a difference between a direction and a destination. If we drive north we do not necessarily want to live at the North Pole.

 # 46   The Sikh religion in India set out to reconcile Islam with Hinduism. One of the main beliefs of Sikhism is that all religions are equally valid and are but different paths to the same god.

In theory we should be tolerant but in practice we are not. If you and I disagree then I must be 'right' and you must be 'wrong'. I shall therefore seek to prove you wrong and, in general, treat you as though you were wrong.

This is the natural discriminatory behaviour of the human brain reinforced by our thinking habits.

It is only too easy to pass from certainty to arrogance to intolerance to persecution.

This is clearly the exact opposite of 'wisdom'.

 # 47   Athletes who compete in races of 1500 metres or over tend to be slight in build. The reason is fairly obvious. If you are larger, then the weight of your body and legs is that much greater. In the course of a 1500-metre race the larger person may be 'lifting' several tonnes more than the light person.

So we set up a 'generalization' that heavy people do not make good distance runners. This would indeed apply to most heavy runners, though there might be an occasional exception.

Generalizations are a sort of box, definition or category. Many of them are true and very useful. You do not have

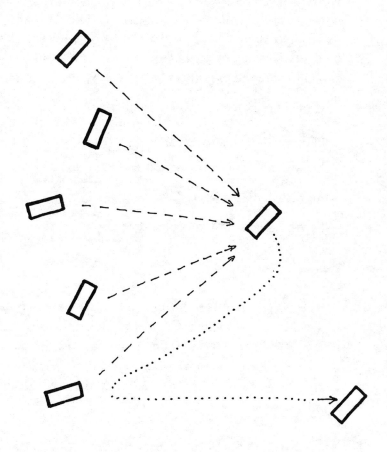

A generalization is a sort of averaging out and is only partly true in each case.

to keep putting your finger into a flame to find that all flames burn.

Then there are other generalizations which are only true most of the time, or part of the time, or even not true at all. These are the prejudices and stereotypes:

– women are not very good at mathematics

– the French make great lovers

– the Africans have a strong sense of rhythm

– the British prefer warm beer

– the Americans have no culture, etc.

———

 # 48   A knife is very useful for cutting up food. A knife may also be used to stab someone. Chemistry makes the medicines that save millions of lives. Chemistry makes the poison gases that have killed thousands. Mathematics makes engineering possible. Mathematics makes the nuclear bomb possible.

Any powerful system can be used for the wrong purposes. Any powerful system can be used badly.

So our habit of 'judgement boxes' is powerful, but can also be dangerous if used badly.

One of the roles of 'wisdom' is to make sure that our judgement-box system of thinking is used sensibly.

———————

 # 49   The key danger of the judgement-box system is arrogance. How can we prevent that shift from useful certainty to dangerous arrogance? We need to use the 'boxes' to help us but not to imprison us.

Wisdom suggests we use terms like 'usually', 'by and large', 'most of the time', 'probably' and 'maybe', instead of the more absolute terms like 'must', 'cannot', 'always' and 'never'. This shift in expression diminishes the danger of arrogance while retaining the utility of the boxes. The shift does, however, weaken the very basis of Aristotelian logic, which demands absolute inclusion or exclusion. The shift is from Aristotelian logic to 'fuzzy logic', where something may be half 'in the box' and half outside.

Where generalizations are going to be helpful we can accept more 'righteousness', but where generalizations are harmful then we need to be much less certain.

 # 50   Another danger of the judgement-box system is that the boxes may be out of date. In a rapidly changing world the boxes derived from the past may not be sufficient to understand the future.

The relative helplessness of the UN in Somalia, Ruanda and Bosnia showed that the principles that had been designed to deal with conflicts between nations did not apply to the breakdown of the nation itself. The thinking was trapped in old-fashioned boxes.

While language is immensely helpful for our thinking, language can also be a dangerous encyclopedia of

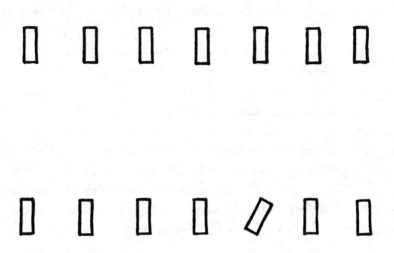

The upper line suggests the blocks are always vertical. In the lower line the blocks are 'usually' vertical.

ignorance. Concepts that were formed in the past, around values and information available at that time, are frozen into permanence in language. Use of these words then forces us to perceive the world in a very old-fashioned way. That is why I am working on a new language for thinking: one that avoids the baggage of the past.

━━━━━━━━━━

 # 51 Labels are a sort of 'box'. Once we slap a label on something then we 'know how to deal with it'. There are the usual simple labels: 'good' or 'bad'; 'right' or 'wrong'; 'true' or 'untrue'; 'useful' or 'useless', etc. Such labels save a lot of thinking. The labels set out a whole perception about something. We look at things through the labels and only notice what agrees with the label.

When students in a class were randomly assigned to two groups, 'promising' and 'slower', they performed according to the label. Teachers given the labels treated students according to the label.

━━━━━━━━━━

 # 52 Adjectives are dangerous. You should usually mistrust anyone who uses a lot of adjectives in an argument. Adjectives are a way of attaching your subjective feeling to something in an attempt to show that the quality is really objective. When you call an artist 'presumptuous' that says much more about you than about the artist. When a critic calls something 'too simple' that says a lot about that critic's need for complexity.

It is part of wisdom to mistrust the use of adjectives. That does not mean that we should remove adjectives from language, but that we should realize that adjectives are usually subjective.

———————————

 # 53 If something is good then more of it must be better. If some money is good then more money is better. If strength is good then more strength is better. If democracy is good then more is better. If intelligence is good then more is better. This is so obvious that we take it for granted. But it can be dangerous and misleading and give rise to many problems.

No salt on food leaves the food tasting insipid. Some salt is good. More salt gives an unpleasant taste. Even more salt makes the food uneatable.

This is obviously a different model or a different metaphor. Is it possible that, if something is 'good', then more is not better but worse?

Some wine apparently reduces the risk of heart attack. More wine may make you drunk and too much may give you cirrhosis of the liver. The Laffer curve (called after the economist Arthur Laffer) suggested that increasing taxation actually reduced the amount collected because people made greater efforts to avoid taxation.

I suspect there is a 'salt curve' for intelligence in a nation. If people are too intelligent then they can spend all their time quarrelling and fighting with each other instead of working constructively together. You could even suggest that unusually good brakes on a car could be dangerous because the car behind would not expect such quick stopping and would run into the back of you.

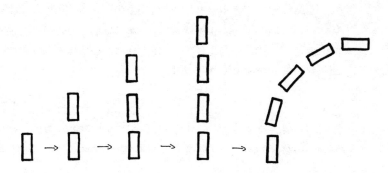

If something is good then surely more is better. But more height may make the tower topple over.

It may even be that too much democracy is a bad thing, because if every shade of opinion has to be taken into account then the system is biased towards doing nothing at all. While this may indeed be the best policy when things are going well it may not be so good when leadership and action are needed.

Just as we need to keep in mind the 'investment' model as well as the 'walking' model (you can only take one road) so we also need to keep in mind the 'salt curve'.

It is very much part of wisdom to have a range of such models in mind. They then become 'possibilities' through which we look at situations.

 # 54   There is also the 'threshold' or 'critical mass' model.

When the inventor of the telephone, Alexander Graham Bell, offered his patents to Western Electric, the invention was dismissed as a 'toy'. Although this seems very silly in hindsight, there was a certain logic to the decision. Until a sufficient number of people had telephones the device was merely a toy to link up two parties. There has to be a 'critical mass'.

Water flooding the street outside your house does not affect your house until the water level rises above the 'threshold'. Then the water starts pouring in. For a long time you may do something with no effect. You may even

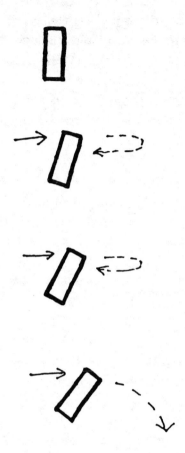

You push on the block but it returns to its position. As you push harder you suddenly reach a point when the block topples over. You have reached the threshold.

give up on the basis that it does not work. Then, suddenly, the effect starts coming through. This applies both to beneficial matters and also to harmful matters. Rumours may have no effect on morale for a long time and then suddenly morale deteriorates. Unemployment may not affect the economy for a time and then suddenly the fear of being unemployed hits spending and planning. Increased spending on education may not have much effect until a threshold has been passed.

Once again, wisdom suggests that you hold 'possibilities' in mind.

 # 55 Truth is one of our great currencies. The intellectual economy depends largely on trading in truth.

The nature of truth seems so very obvious: truth is the opposite of 'untruth'. We can recognize 'untruth' and therefore we know what truth is. Of course we do not know.

There is game 'truth', where you set up a game and then you abide by the rules. If you play tennis, or chess, or democracy, or the judicial system, then you play by the rules. Truth is what accords with the rules you have 'chosen' to follow.

Then there is 'checking truth', which means that you can check things out for yourself. You can do your own checking as in measurement or science. You can rely on the checking done by others as in following a tide table (to determine when you can enter harbour). This could also

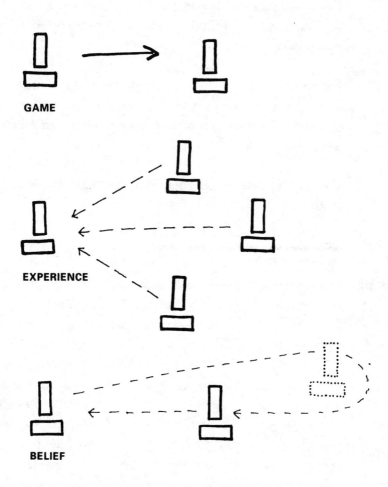

GAME

EXPERIENCE

BELIEF

In the first type of truth you set up the game and then you follow the rules.

In the second type of truth you check out whether things are as you suppose.

In the third type of truth your belief changes your perceptions so that they reinforce the belief.

be called 'experience' truth because you, or someone else, has actually experienced these things. There is, however, a subjective element about experience which could be misleading.

Finally there is 'belief' truth. You believe something to be true. This belief truth may so affect your perception that you see things in such a way as to reinforce that belief truth.

Wisdom involves understanding the different sorts of truth.

 # 56 Science uses something called 'proto-truth', except that it is never called by that name. Every scientist believes, like Plato, that he or she has discovered the ultimate inner truth of matters. Academics can be very fierce indeed in their defence of such 'truth' and their attack on other people's 'truth'. Yet history has shown again and again that what was firmly held as truth turns out not to be so at all. So science is really dealing with 'proto-truth'. A proto-truth is a truth we hold to be true for practical pur-poses – provided we are simultaneously trying to change it. Without such proto-truth we would just sit back and say that everything was illusion and unknowable – as some cultures have chosen to do. The great Socrates had little time for science and regarded it as a waste of time.

 # 57 It is not difficult to feel that you 'are right' or that you 'have the truth'. Truth is as much an emotion as an objective fact. When the nerve circuits in the brain achieve a certain 'circularity' then we have the emotion of truth. This is reasonable and essential for practical purposes. We could never get on with life without this 'biological' emotion of truth.

Wisdom needs to recognize the reality and nature of circular perceptual truth.

 # 58 Humility is the opposite of arrogance. How do you know that you do not know something that you should know? Only humility will tell you that there is a 'possibility' of something you need to know but do not yet know. Only humility will tell you that there is the 'possibility' of alternatives you have not yet generated.

Humility is the opening up of probes and communication with the world around, just as arrogance is the cutting off of communication.

 # 59 If we contrast the habits of wisdom with the habits of our traditional judgement-box thinking system we might find the following:

Instead of a single 'truth' we have parallel possibilities.

Instead of judgement we have design (putting things together to achieve our purpose).

Instead of boxes we have values.

Instead of the 'discover' idiom we have the 'create' idiom.

You can dig for gold by removing all the soil and then washing the nugget under a tap. You can 'discover' gold.

But you do not 'discover' a house. You have to design the house and build it.

Wisdom is more about 'designing a way forward' than about 'discovering the truth'.

There are problems which can be solved by discovering the cause and removing that cause.

There are problems where the cause cannot be found or cannot be removed. In such cases we need to 'design' a way forward leaving the cause in place.

In general, we are very much better at analysis than at design.

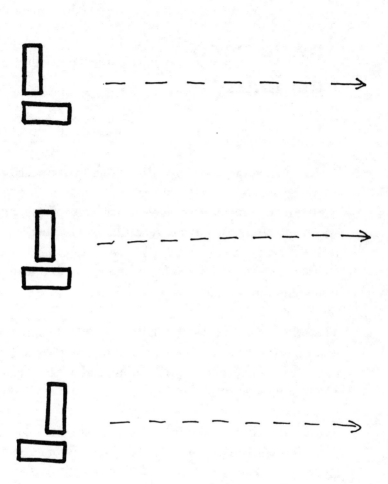

We accept and follow parallel possibilities. We do not have to decide which is right and which is wrong.

The Power of Possibility

 # 60   There are two aspects to wisdom. The first aspect is to know how to deal with difficulties, problems and bad habits. In this respect we need to be wary of the 'edge effect' and the difficulty of reconciling the 'now' needs with the longer-term benefits. We also need to be aware of the dangers of the judgement-box system with its sometimes false certainty and arrogance.

The other aspect is to put some emphasis on those very important aspects of perception and thinking which have not really been given their proper attention. Prime amongst these is 'possibility'.

'Possibility' leads to creativity, the generation of alternatives, thought experiments, hypotheses and excursions into 'Yonder Park' (the future).

Where progress does not happen by accident it usually happens through the generation and exploration of possibilities.

———

 # 61   We do not like 'possibilities' for very good reasons. Possibilities are the opposite of certainty. We need to make

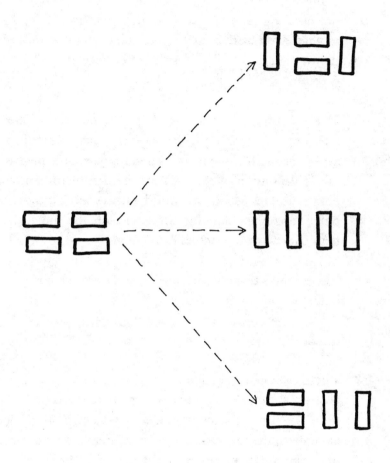

The pieces could be arranged in a number of different ways. All of these are possibilities.

practical decisions. Possibility leaves open the risk of danger: this berry 'might' be good to eat. Possibility does not offer a guaranteed reward: this road 'might' lead you to where you want to go. So possibility is not attractive to the human mind. How much better is clear and defined certainty.

Then 'possibility' opens up all sorts of nonsense. Science has forever been trying to flee from superstitious nonsense. 'Possibility' seems to suggest that any fanciful theory has a validity. Maybe there are hidden 'spirits' moving atoms around. Maybe the world is flat. Maybe the world is balanced on the shoulder of Atlas. Maybe the sun is a fiery chariot drawn across the sky.

The irony is that the driving force of science has indeed been the 'possibility' system.

—

 # 62 There is evidence. Then someone comes along and creates a possibility. This is the 'hypothesis' that has been the driving force of science. That hypothesis gives us something to work towards. The hypothesis directs the search for more evidence and for the design of experiments.

The expectation that the hypothesis is going to be critically attacked drives the search for better supporting evidence. But the critical destruction of a hypothesis does not produce a better one. A better hypothesis is produced by the creative effort of someone who comes along with a new hypothesis as a possibility.

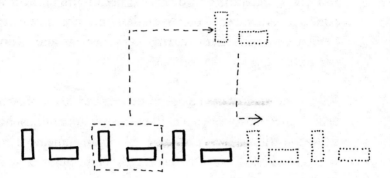

We make a guess as to how the pattern will continue. This is a hypothesis.
It allows us to predict future behaviour.

Chinese technology was very far advanced two thousand years ago and way ahead of the West. It is said that progress then came to a dead end because the academics concerned themselves only with description (as in so many fields today). It seems that the Chinese never developed the concept of the 'hypothesis'.

Just as the hypothesis has been the driving force of Western science, so the driving force of Western technology has been the 'dream' or 'vision'. We can imagine where we want to be. That is the possibility. Now, how do we get there?

 # 63 A chicken is separated by a wire-mesh fence from a bowl of chicken food on the other side of the fence. The chicken tries harder and harder to get to the food which is so temptingly 'there'. The chicken starves to death within sight of the food.

A dog is separated by a wire-mesh fence from a bone on the other side of the fence. Like the chicken the dog tries to get through or under the fence. Then comes the difference. The dog moves away from the tempting bone to explore. The dog moves along the fence and finds that the fence is limited. The dog steps round the fence and gets the food.

Was the dog being logical? Was there any reason to suppose the fence to be limited? The great dingo fence in Australia runs for thousands of miles. We can say that the dog was exploring. The dog was curious. The result of that curiosity-driven exploration was success.

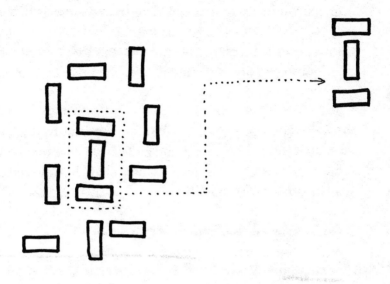

A hypothesis is a structured guess that we impose on a situation. It may not be at all obvious. We have to create the possibility in our minds.

There are bees in a bottle which is placed with its bottom end towards the sunlight. The bees try and try to move directly towards the sunlight. They never succeed.

If the bees are replaced by flies then the flies, like the dog, set out to explore and emerge from the open neck of the bottle.

It would be anthropomorphic to suggest that the dog and the flies were bringing to mind and considering the 'possibility' of another approach. It was probably no more than a 'habit of exploration'.

Considering 'possibilities' is itself no more than a habit of exploration. The only difference is that we explore things in our minds. We do 'thought experiments' just as Einstein did thought experiments.

 # 64 When you set out to look for alternatives do you 'know' that there are any alternatives to be found? Do you know that you are going to be able to find those alternatives? There is no certainty at all. There may not even be a hint that there are alternatives.

You believe in the 'possibility' of there being alternatives.

In fact, there are three levels of possibility:

1. That there are indeed alternatives

2. That you will be able to find (or design) them

3. That they will be suitable.

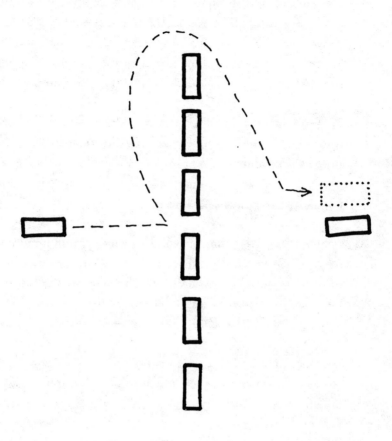

When the head-on approach does not work you have to explore new approaches.

When you set up a 'po' provocation in lateral thinking, do you know that you are going to get a useful idea from it? Of course not. There is only the possibility. ('Po' is a word I invented to signal a provocation which is a statement we know not to be true but use in order to stimulate new thoughts. See *Po: Beyond Yes and No*, Penguin 1990.)

When a hunter goes hunting does he or she know that there will be game? There is only the possibility, sometimes a probability.

 # 65 It is extraordinary that the whole business of 'possibility' is so poorly treated, if at all, at university or any other level of education. There is this totally absurd notion that knowledge proceeds by neat steps from known facts through logical deduction to further knowledge.

This is not only contrary to experience but also contrary to the behaviour of any self-organizing information system.

The explanation could be simple. Historically universities descended from colleges of theology and law, and in those areas logical games with words are often sufficient.

It is very much part of wisdom to understand the power and the use of possibility.

 # 66 Traditional science insists that we set up the most reasonable hypothesis and then, according to Karl Popper, seek to demolish that hypothesis. This process works but is very slow and inefficient. The evidence is looked at through the most reasonable hypothesis. When this collapses we seek another. The process is sequential.

It is far better to have several parallel hypotheses which are held at the same time – even including some more speculative ones. This way, if the hypothesis turns out to be incorrect then there are others that are being worked upon in parallel. It also means that the same person can look at the evidence through different organizing windows.

There is an art and a craft in setting up hypotheses. Scientists, and others, need to be taught this craft.

 # 67 The legal system would probably be unworkable if lawyers developed a high skill in creativity. In many countries a jury cannot convict if there is a 'reasonable doubt'.

From almost any set of evidence a creative lawyer should be able to create a reasonable doubt.

Once the 'possibility' has been suggested then it cannot be unthought. That possibility now has to be discounted in some way. So the creative lawyer produces another possibility. Producing possibilities is, on balance, probably easier than discounting them.

 # 68 Add up the numbers from 1 to 10. That is easy enough.

Now add up the numbers from 1 to 100. That is also easy but tedious and time-consuming. You know the way to do it. Would you consider there was a possibility of a much simpler way to do it? There is a way to do it in five seconds. You have to believe in that sort of possibility in order to go looking for a simpler way.

X { Do we only go looking for better ways to do things when there is a problem or when the present way is obviously unsatisfactory? That is the current and very limited view of 'improvement'.

There should be a willingness to use creativity everywhere and to seek out better ways of doing things and better concepts. This applies also to areas where we are very happy and complacent about our current methods.

The sense of 'possibility' is the great motivator for creative people.

 # 69 Of a group of eleven Nobel prize laureates only one had arrived at his or her breakthrough idea through systematic analysis. In all the other instances the idea had been triggered by mistake, by anomaly or by speculation.

Play and provocation are ways of upsetting the world within or outside our minds so that new things can happen and be observed.

We now know that there is a logical, mathematical need for both creativity and provocation in any self-organizing system – like the human brain.

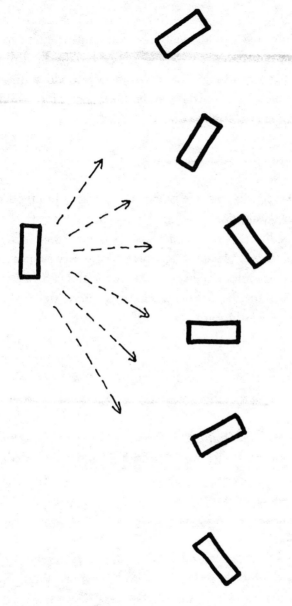

We can generate a large number of alternatives and possibilities which are connected in one way or another.

It is very much part of wisdom to know this and to know that experience, analysis and judgement are simply insufficient. Far too many 'clever' people still believe that information and analysis are enough. That is why progress in many areas is so very slow.

 # 70 Some people do a jigsaw puzzle by starting at one corner and then systematically moving outwards from that one corner. Others lay out all the pieces and then start at several different places. There may be some defined shape in the design and it is easy to work around that shape. So there are many focuses of development. Eventually all the separate pieces fit together.

When you are driving to a new destination you may find that segments of the road are familiar. It then becomes a matter of getting from one familiar segment to another.

We can work possibilities in the same way. We can set up a number of possibilities and then find that some of them do 'click' together.

 # 71 Creativity is a key area in itself. The word 'creativity' is rather too broad in scope and also has an artistic flavouring. That is why I invented the term 'lateral thinking' specifically to cover changes in concepts and perception. The tools and methods of lateral thinking are based directly on the behaviour of the brain as a self-organizing information system which sets up asymmetric patterns.

Lateral thinking is concerned with 'moving laterally across' these patterns.

On a simpler level, you cannot dig a hole in a different place by digging the same hole deeper. Lateral thinking means trying out different perceptions, concepts and approaches instead of trying harder with the traditional ones.

The techniques of lateral thinking are described in other books of mine (see *Lateral Thinking*, Penguin 1990; *Serious Creativity*, HarperCollins 1992).

Wisdom also means knowing when and how to use creativity.

 # 72 There is the generative and productive side of creativity. There is also another side. The ability to generate alternatives is the best counter to arrogance. By putting forward new possibilities as alternatives of explanation or action you show that the one approach offered is not the only one available. At least this offered approach must now show its merit by comparison with other possibilities.

When someone comes to you to say: 'There are only two ways of doing this,' you suggest that there may, possibly, be others.

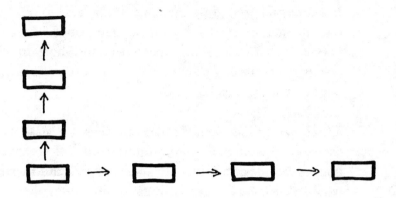

Vertical thinking is building on the same base. Lateral thinking is to do with changing the basic concepts and perceptions.

 # 73 Certainty, probability, possibility and fantasy are all points along one spectrum. Possibility is not the same as fantasy. It is a possibility that we may one day be able to send an instant analysis of our breath or blood down the telephone line. It is a fantasy that we could transport our bodies down the line. There may come a day when that fantasy is also a possibility.

There was a time when the idea of a man setting foot on the moon was no more than a fantasy. The idea that millions of people at home could actually watch this happen would have been even more fantastic.

Possibility is related to current contexts. Possibility does not simply mean 'everything is possible, so anything goes'. Such an attitude diminishes the power of possibility.

It should be noted that 'provocations', as used in lateral thinking, are quite different from possibilities. A provocation may be knowingly wrong, impossible or contradictory and yet provoke valuable ideas. Provocations are not hypotheses.

Wisdom also means knowing how far towards fantasy to take 'possibilities'. There needs to be a conscious decision as to the range of possibilities: how far from the probable and how near to the fantastic?

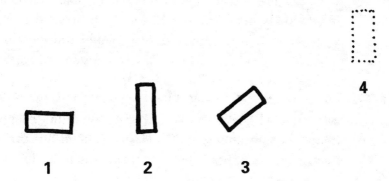

1. Certainty is secure.

2. Probability is less secure.

3. Possibility is only a possibility.

4. Fantasy means only that we can imagine it.

Values

 # 74 The purpose of thinking is to arrange our internal world and external world so as to serve and improve our values. The purpose of action is to put that thinking into effect.

 # 75 It is a function of wisdom to be aware of all the different values involved in a situation. It is a function of wisdom to become aware of the different values of the different parties involved in a situation. It is a function of wisdom to have some sort of priority of values so that the most important ones get proper attention. It is a function of wisdom to design action so as to satisfy as many values as possible. It is a function of wisdom consciously to trade off one value against another when both cannot be satisfied.

Wisdom should be the architecture of values. How do we arrange the 'value space'?

 # 76 There are cultural values, local values and family values. These are things we are supposed to do and principles we are supposed to follow. Much of the time we go along with these · expectations because such values have indeed

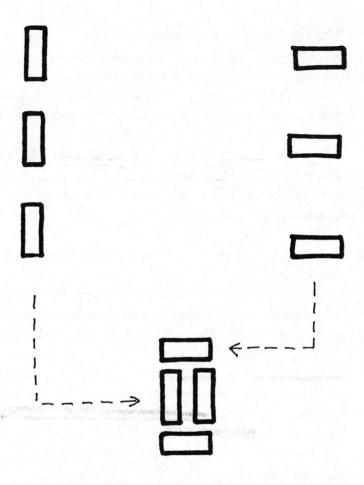

In any situation there are many values involved. There is a need to combine the different values.

become our values or because we fear group disapproval if we do not.

There are spiritual values and religious values. These may be highly personal or more overt. Such values determine whether we feel virtuous or guilty. Such values make decisions easier. We do not judge an alternative on its internal merit but look to see if it fits the appropriate values.

There are material values and 'achievement' values. These have a direct value and an indirect one because they may lead to 'recognition', 'power' and 'status', which are also values.

There are less obvious values such as 'boredom', 'interest' and 'hassle'.

There are the basic personal values of emotions, feelings, desires and enjoyment.

 # 77 The positive values drive our perception and action. These values sensitize the mind and determine how we are going to see things. The smell of food has a higher value if you are hungry.

It is important to realize that values do not just come in during the design of action or at the moment of choice. Values determine how we see things in the first place.

When you are frightened every strange noise is interpreted by perception as a potential problem.

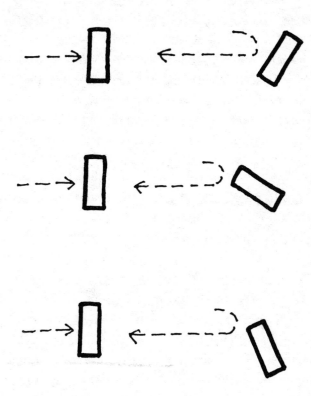

There are positive values which we go towards and seek out. There are negative values which we try to avoid and reject.

The negative values are the ones we seek to avoid. We seek to avoid pain, discomfort, humiliation, hassle, bad taste, embarrassment, etc.

We seek to avoid insecurity. But we also seek to achieve security. Is security just the absence of 'insecurity'? The two are not mirror images. We can seek to avoid insecurity. We can also positively seek out security. We can seek to be free of tyranny. But we can also seek more 'freedom' as such even when there is no tyranny.

---

78   Where do values come from?

There are supposed to be some innate human values such as respect for life, love of a child, sense of justice (fairness), spiritual nourishment. These are supposed to be universal. Nevertheless, such fundamental values as respect for life seem to vary from culture to culture. Some of the world's greatest civilizations were not averse to exposing weak or, sometimes, female children on hillsides to die. In the past in Japan a midwife would wrap an unwanted child in a mat and kneel on it until it expired.

Even countries with a high degree of respect for human life construct powerful weapons of war specifically to destroy human life (in self-defence) and consider it proper to take human life in the justice system.

At some point values are set by religious beliefs. These may be set formally as part of the religious faith and may be adopted by individual spirituality.

There are also values which are temporarily created by clubs, groups or the demands of fashion.

---

79   In my book *I am Right, You are Wrong*, I tell the story of a mother who is wheeling along two young children in a pram. A neighbour stops the mother to admire the children.

'Don't bother about them,' says the mother. 'You should see the photographs. They are really beautiful.'

In a sense the mother was right. The children would grow up and become bald, wrinkled and paunchy. The photographs would remain beautiful for a very long time.

The purpose of reality is to fuel those myths, stories and beliefs which give value to life. In this respect it is up to us to create values.

A person who takes up a hobby or sets out to collect something is investing in the creation of value. A person who develops a fine taste in wine or an eye for paintings is also investing in value creation.

The person who pays close attention to the taste of the wine is investing in value in a richer experience brought about by a deliberate act of 'attention directing'. This is as deliberate an act of investment as investing in a company or planting bulbs in the garden or spending hours on some course.

 # 80 Values give purpose, meaning, enjoyment and 'value' to life. We can also become hostage to our values, just as we can become hostage to our desires.

Excitement is a value and we may become addicted to seeking out excitement. We may become adrenaline junkies and take up bungee jumping.

Even when we do not actively seek out excitement we may be driven by the desire to avoid 'boredom', which is a very powerful negative value.

Simplicity is a high value, which we may seek directly, or indirectly through a distaste for complications and hassle.

 # 81 It is the task of wisdom to understand values in perception; in the design of action; in making choices and in judgement. What are the values that are driving us? What are the values we shall enjoy at the end? What negative values have we avoided? What value changes have we inflicted on others?

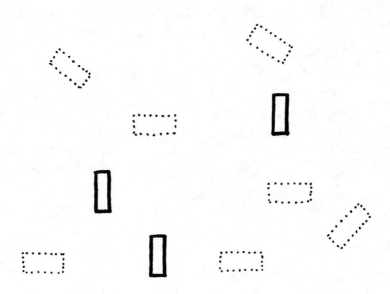

Values give meaning, importance and significance to things. We pick out
and attend to things because they have value.

 # 82   Some people are so violently seasick that they really wish to die. There seems to be no higher value than getting on to firm land. When they have been on firm land for a day or so they do not go around appreciating the firmness of the land.

When you have a violent headache there is no higher value than an aspirin. When the headache is gone then aspirin has a minor security value.

So there are values of the moment and values that are more permanent.

Any 'need' of the moment is a value. If you are thirsty and have a bottle of soft drink but no opener, then a bottle opener has a high value. If you are playing poker and need a certain card to complete a 'full house', then that card has high value.

━━━━━━━━━

 # 83   Not all people have the same needs at the same time. Not all people have the same values. To a union negotiator there is value in the outcome of the negotiation. There is even more value in how his performance is going to look to the union members. An agreement that is reached too early may be less stressful and less financially painful to everyone involved but may give the impression that the outcome was not sufficiently contested. A better deal might have been obtained if more time had been taken in disagreement.

Appearance values are important in politics, in business and in birds. In many bird species the female is attracted

Values give purpose to life. Values set objectives and the reason for doing things. Without values there is drift.

to the male purely by looks: a long feather or a bright red breast. There is no question of strength, of speed of wing or of being a good 'provider'. Appearance is enough. It seems to work well. Birds survive and prosper.

Because different parties have different values, the skill of a negotiator is to seek, through design, to produce an outcome which accommodates as many of the different values as possible.

Negotiation becomes more difficult when one party has as a prime value that the other party must suffer. This deliberate win–lose attitude makes win–win design impossible.

Negotiation should be a design process with new alternatives being put forward. It need not be a matter of pressuring the acceptance of the existing alternatives. Negotiation does not have to be an auction of pain.

───────────

84 It is said that Napoleon found it cheaper to reward his men with medals rather than with more money. Recognition and honour are powerful motivators. They are powerful values.

When General Electric (USA) asked its research workers what they wanted most, it was not more money or more time off, it was 'recognition' for their efforts and successes.

Considering how cheap this sort of value is to give, it is surprising we do not use it more. It is also one of those

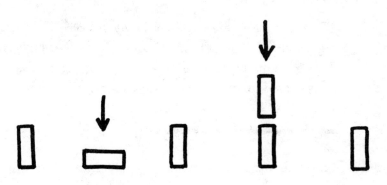

Within a group different people have a different value, just as in a play actors have different roles.

values which you can give without in any way diminishing the supply.

There is the very high value of being noticed. There is the high value of 'being given attention'. It might even be said that 'love' in its receiving aspects is no more than an exaggerated form of 'being given attention'.

 # 85 The Italians have a great 'group culture'. They meet together. They go out to dinner in large groups. Everyone in the group has an accepted and understood position. There is not the jockeying for power or attention that there is in so many other countries. There is in the group the 'jester', who is always trying to make people laugh. There is the person who simply contributes by laughing loudly and regularly. There is the person everyone teases affectionately. There is the 'wise' guy, who is supposed to know everything. It is like a large family.

There is high value in the sense of 'belonging'. Youngsters start smoking in order to belong to the 'gang'. Drugs are tried in the same way.

The English emphasis on 'class' and 'club' is an excellent device for the protection of mediocrity. If you are stupid you can still belong and will be protected by the others. If you try to be too smart, that is frowned upon because you are setting competitive standards for the others. 'Showing off' is not permitted for the same reason. Once you 'belong', you are carried along and do not have to make much effort.

Belonging to the gang is important because it is terrible to be left out of any gang; the terror of isolation is real when all action goes through the gangs. You also acquire your identity and your mates by belonging.

 # 86 I once suggested (see *Handbook for the Positive Revolution*, Penguin 1992) that young women had it in their power to change the values of society. Young men want to show off to young women. Young men want to impress young women. So if young women were to down-value aggression and antisocial behaviour then these types of behaviour would soon go out of fashion.

This is a moderately sensible idea and could be powerful. But it is not likely to happen. The younger girls, aged fourteen or fifteen, are on the edge of being able to join the gang. These girls want to be accepted by the gang as soon as possible. So they not only accept the existing gang values but actually show high enthusiasm in order to gain acceptance. So they are never going to be agents for change.

 # 87 Someone with 'good taste' finds it very hard to believe that someone else can really have 'bad taste'. Is it perhaps just an insensitivity or lack of any taste at all?

Aesthetics are intangible but very real values. A scientist has an aesthetic feeling that the explanation is too complex. An ecologist has an aesthetic feeling that the proposed action is going to be damaging to the environment. Politicians are guided by their own aesthetic political sensitivities all the time. Aesthetics in art and architecture are a matter of fashion, culture and, perhaps, some innate properties of the human mind.

 # 88   It is sometimes said that the 'Slav' temperament cherishes a 'good anguish'. Happiness is not durable. It is there one day but next day it is gone. Anguish is much more durable. You can nurture and polish a good anguish. It will not let you down. Hatred gives a permanent focus and mission to life. The emotion is even enjoyable.

Love is a general value stimulator. Love makes food taste better, your neighbour more tolerable and the sun shine brighter.

 # 89   It is part of wisdom to know that logic never changes love. Logic never changes any emotion or feeling. You can spend hours with logical argument trying to change some feeling or prejudice. You are not likely to succeed.

But perception can change feelings and emotions. If you put forward a 'possible' way of looking at the situation, then perception can change and with it the feeling. If it is suggested that someone is 'trying to make you jealous' because he or she loves you, then you see the flirtatious behaviour differently.

paradox

So where do feelings come in? If you start off with an emotion, that will fashion your perception and limit it. If your perception triggers an emotion, then that will also limit your perception. Feelings should come in at the end

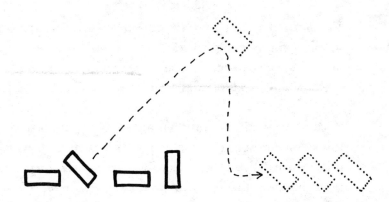

A feeling arising from a situation may change our perception so that now we see the situation only through that feeling.

in order to judge the situation or help design the appropriate action.

In a normal argument or discussion you are not supposed to allow your feelings to come in because argument is all about objective logic. Of course, feelings come in anyway – you just disguise them as logic.

Because feelings and intuition are so important a part of thinking, the Six Hats method, which is now so widely used around the world (see *Six Thinking Hats*, Penguin 1987), allocates the 'Red Hat' to the expression of feelings. When the Red Hat is in use everyone is free to express his or her feelings without justification and without apology.

There is a value in having feelings and a value in having them known.

#**90**   There is a table with three glasses on it. One is a glass of milk. One is a glass of beer. One is a glass of orange juice. If you have very bad eyesight and can only see the table as a blur then you cannot exert your values in choosing the drink you want. If you put on spectacles and improve your eyesight then you can see all three glasses and you choose according to your value.

That is what the CoRT thinking lessons, now widely used in schools, are designed to do: improve perception so youngsters can apply their values (see p. 41).

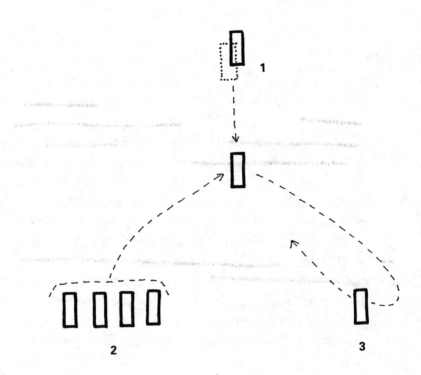

There are different sources of values:

1. Innate and basic human values;

2. Values set by groups and cultures;

3. Belief-based values.

 # 91 Wisdom is very much concerned with values in the following ways:

Awareness

There is a need to be aware of all the different values involved in the situation. There are the values of the acting parties and also the values of those likely to be affected by the action. There are the obvious values and the ones you have to search for. You need to have in mind a wide range of 'positive values' in order to recognize them. It is like bird-watching. You will not recognize that bird unless you have had previous experience with that shape. That is why this section has laid out various value possibilities. Values do not declare themselves. You have to notice and attend to them. There are the positive and negative values. There are the values that 'drive' the situation and there are the values that are used mainly for 'assessment'. A wise person is able to develop a good value 'map'.

Important Values

Not all values are equally important. Some are 'essential' and some are 'luxury' values. It would be good to have the luxury values but there is an absolute need to have the essential values. For example, in some cultures it is an essential value that a negotiating party does not 'lose face'. Between the two extremes of essential and luxury there is a spectrum. There is skill in deciding where the other values are placed along this spectrum.

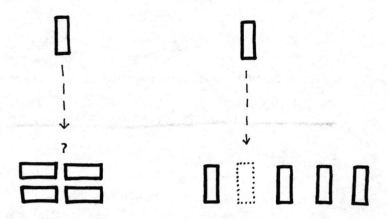

If your values do not fit the world around you then you can try to rearrange
the world – as missionaries do.

Design

Values are the essential drivers of design. The purpose of the design is to serve the values. It is no use designing a bed that is not comfortable to sleep upon. Your design may start by following the thrust of some key values. Then you seek to modify the design to accommodate other values. There are different ways in which values can be fed into a design. It is not possible to have all the values operating at every stage.

Reconcile

How can competing values and contrary values be reconciled? This may apply to your own thinking and almost always applies in negotiation. There is a great need for creative design in reconciling values. It has to be a creative process. Analysis and judgement will never achieve such reconciliation. They are concerned with the superiority of one value over another.

Trade-off

When design has not succeeded in reconciling different values or accommodating different values there may have to be a 'trade-off'. In buying a car, you may have to decide between 'appearance' and 'fuel consumption' because there are no good-looking cars with a low fuel consumption. In choosing a husband you may have to decide between excitement and earning capacity. Trade-offs should always be conscious. It is never a matter of ignoring, neglecting or discarding a value. There should be a conscious decision to give up one value in exchange for another one (trading).

Assessment

Values come directly into play in our choice of car, wife, course of action, strategy, etc. Part of our assessment is based on whether the suggestion will work at all, part on the cost and investment needed. The rest is on the 'fit' between the suggestion and our needs and values. When a choice or decision has been made it is useful to spell out the reasons behind that choice or decision: 'I have made this choice because . . .'

You may find that the actual value driving the decision is not a key value at all. For example, you may make a major decision 'in order to avoid upsetting' someone. That is the edge effect in action.

Prediction

Values are a key part of prediction. If you want to know how some person or some party is going to act, then you need to know the driving values. If you want to know how some suggestion is going to be accepted, then you need to know the driving values. If you want to know how things are going to develop in the world, you need to have some idea of the driving values.

Changing Values

Values change. Some values come into fashion, others die out. It is important to be aware of the changing values.

Wisdom is a matter of knowing what the values are, how to cope with them and how to use them.

 # 92 A simple way to sort out values is to draw four broad columns. In the second column you write down all the values you can think of in the situation. This includes positive and negative values, personal and 'other people' values.

You now go down the list and transfer to the first column all the values that are peripheral or unimportant.

You now go down the list a second time and transfer to the third column the 'more important' values.

Finally, you go down the third column and transfer to the fourth column what you consider to be the 'essential' values.

Now look over all the columns and see if they make sense. Make adjustments as required.

Matrix?

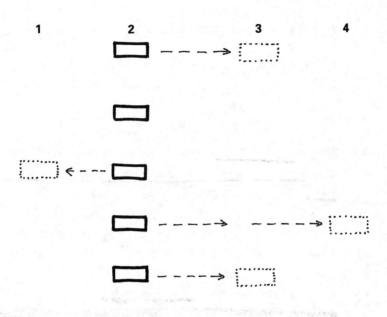

You put down all the values you can think of in column 2 and then transfer some of them to the other columns: to column 1 those things which are unimportant; to column 3 the more important values; to column 4 the 'essential' values which must be taken into account.

Contrary and Contradiction

 # 93 The Gang of Three, and Socrates in particular, insisted that in order to seek the truth we must remove the 'untruth'. This means that in order to get a change we must attack the present method or system. We must show that it is wrong. In lawcourts with an adversarial system you must prove the other side wrong.

This method has two unfortunate effects. The first is that you are forced to attack something which you do not believe to be bad. You are forced to seem 'against' it.

A young lady who has difficulty in choosing between two suitors is often advised to choose the one she prefers and then, in her mind, to focus on all the bad things about the other one. This will rid her mind of the indecision.

The second unfortunate effect is that it is very difficult to say: 'This is excellent and very useful – but not good enough.'

If a car has only three of the four tyres inflated, you do not need to attack the inflated tyres in order to point out that they are inadequate.

We should not be forced to attack as bad something which

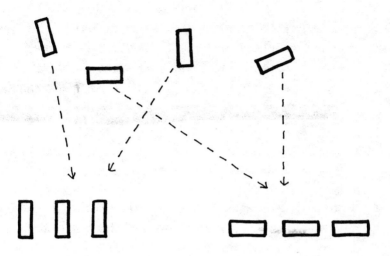

In order to make sense of a complex world we put things into boxes, definitions and categories. This makes it easier to recognize things. We owe this to Aristotle of the Gang of Three.

is not. We should be able to acknowledge that something is good but inadequate.

I believe the thinking system formulated by the Greek Gang of Three is excellent – but not good enough. It is not so applicable in a changing world and it has insufficient generating and design capacity. The danger lies not in the system itself but in those who believe it to be sufficient.

 # 94 In legislative assemblies and parliaments the opposition feels obliged to give the impression that what the government does is stupid, unfair and possibly corrupt. The government is obliged to feel the same about the opposition.

Increasingly, the general public do not go along with the necessities of this childish game. They do not believe that everything the government does is bad and must be opposed. Nor do they believe that the government has all the best ideas. In areas like economics there is a growing convergence. There are sensible things to do about inflation and about stimulating employment – and both sides will do the same things.

Do people accept that this is 'the game' and this is how politics must always be played? Does wisdom separate the game from reality? Or, does wisdom consider it a silly game?

Wisdom may become increasingly impatient with the crude oppositional model, whether it is in government or in family discussions.

Wisdom may require a shift to the more constructive idiom of parallel thinking. Here different views, values and suggestions are put down in parallel. There is then a joint effort to design a way forward. The powerful Six Hats framework (see *Six Thinking Hats*, Penguin 1987) has been rapidly taken up by businesses around the world because it provides an escape from traditional argument. It also reduces meeting times by up to 75 per cent.

 # 95 Aristotle's first principle was that something had to be either 'in the box' or 'outside the box' and could not be half in and half out. The boxes refer to definitions or categories. Someone had to have measles or not have measles. You could not have half-measles.

The second principle was that something had to be in the box or outside the box – there was nowhere else it could be.

From these principles arose the principle of 'mutual exclusivity'. Two mutually exclusive things could not both be true – that would be a contradiction.

This simplified thinking and gave a useful logic in some instances and a false logic in others.

From this horror of contradiction arose some polarities. There was 'true' and 'untrue'. Untrue became 'false'. There was 'right' and 'not right'. Not right became 'wrong'.

Very soon we were dealing with apparent opposites: peace or excitement; stability or change; conservative or radical.

Although some of these polarities are not strict contradictions, they have the same effect as saying that you cannot have both.

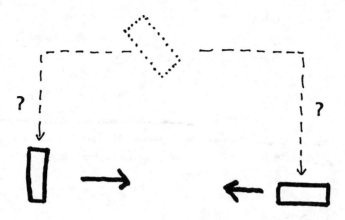

Sometimes we have to argue about whether something really fits into one standard box or another.

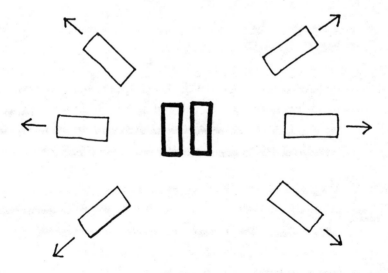

Ever since Socrates (of the Gang of Three), we have believed that if we only remove the 'untruth' we will be left with the wonderful truth. So criticism may be sufficient.

 # 96 The Japanese were not much influenced by the Gang of Three and therefore have little trouble holding both sides of a contradiction at the same time. Every day at lunch leaders of the motor industry meet in their club and discuss mutual problems. As soon as they leave the club they are fierce rivals. They see no problem at all in someone being a friend and an un-friend (enemy) at the same time. The Japanese also had no difficulty taking up 'fuzzy logic', when many intellectuals in the USA (where it was invented) rejected it as being contrary to Aristotle's principles.

Whether as a pure contradiction, as a dichotomy or as a polarization, we are so often put in an either/or situation. We are asked to choose one or the other. Logic is said to depend upon this. But wisdom is different.

 # 97 At the beginning of this book the either/or 'walking' model was contrasted with the 'portfolio' model. We need to be on our guard when asked to use the 'walking' model. There are times when this is totally inappropriate.

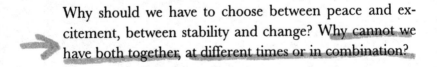

Why should we have to choose between peace and excitement, between stability and change? Why cannot we have both together, at different times or in combination?

 # 98 There are a number of practical strategies we can use for dealing with contradictions or contrary values.

ACCEPT

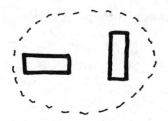

COMBINE

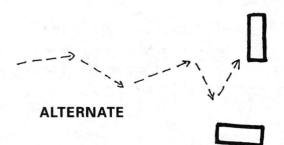

ALTERNATE

There are different things we can do with contradictions:

1. we can accept both without getting upset;

2. we can seek to combine them;

3. we can alternate back and forth between them.

Accept Both

Just as the Japanese can conceive of a friend/enemy, we should be able to conceive of an honest thief, a good poor deal or a fast slow car. When we accept both sides our minds then seek to understand this in practical terms. A fast slow car might be a slow car with fast acceleration. A good poor deal is a sound deal which does not offer as many benefits as had been expected.

Combine Them

This is a deliberate design process. Can we combine the contrary values? Combining peace and excitement may mean seeking excitement from a stable base or seeking excitement in a way which does not threaten the stable base.

Alternate

This means switching from one value to the contrary value and back again. You can be sensitive at times and ruthless at other times. You can be conservative about some things and radical about others.

Parallel Thinking

Design usually requires that a range of values is kept in mind the whole time. These values exert their influence at different points. For example, there might be the contrary values of 'low cost' and 'luxury'. The result may be a

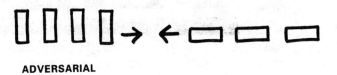

ADVERSARIAL

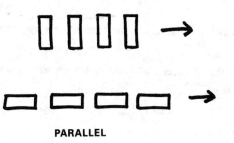

PARALLEL

Traditional adversarial thinking means that opposing points of view must battle against each other. Parallel thinking means that the opposing points of view can work constructively and cooperatively in parallel.

low-cost house with touches that suggest luxury. Parallel thinking requires that both sides of a contradiction and opposing values are accepted and laid down in parallel. There is no need to make a choice between them. The design stage can take them both into account. Judgement cannot proceed on this basis but design can.

 # 99 We believe that we should have only one strategy. Why? There can be multiple strategies, all of which are pursued at the same time. We accept that we should have only one belief system. Why? Why not have a number of belief systems in parallel? There are times when you are forced to decide – as in the walking model – but we should not assume that this is always the case. We can have the dual strategy of making a choice when required and not making a choice when this is not required.

There are times when you may need to think fast. There are times when you would do better to think very slowly. You do not have to choose a middle speed. You can think fast part of the time and think slowly when this is more appropriate.

Just as different foods require different methods of cooking, so different situations require different approaches. It is not a matter of deciding which approach is 'your style' and then only using this one approach.

 # 100 Wisdom involves avoiding those harsh rules which we force upon ourselves because they are useful in some situations. We can acknowledge that usefulness in those situations and develop other behaviour for other situations. Behaviour can be situation-dependent rather than ego-dependent.

Hostage, Slave, Prisoner and Puppet

 # 101 William Harvey, who discovered the circulation of the blood in the human body, suspected that he had an aneurysm of the aorta (a weakening and ballooning of the main blood vessel emerging from the heart). He used to say: 'I am at the mercy of any ruffian who chooses to make me lose my temper.'

He knew that if he lost his temper his blood pressure would rise and the aneurysm might burst, so killing him. So anyone had this power over him, the power to make him lose his temper – which was, apparently, not very difficult.

 # 102 We overreact to things. People can make us lose our tempers.

In many relationships one partner or the other, or both, learn the 'hot buttons' to press. If you press these hot buttons you get an overreaction. Partners learn how to get a reaction from each other. There are certain remarks to make, certain things to touch upon, and reason is replaced by emotional overreaction. A husband might make comparisons with his mother's cooking. A wife might make remarks about her husband's virility.

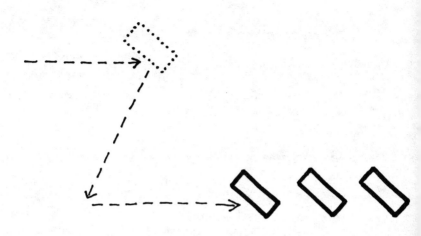

We are all hostages to our emotions, which set our perceptions. So we react to the world we see through those perceptions which are determined by the emotions of the moment. We are free to be trapped by emotions.

The small triggers are known to set off a considerable response.

A person who loses his temper easily is hostage to that emotion. That person is also hostage to another person who knows how to make him lose his temper. Hostage means not being in charge. Hostage means subject to the will of another.

 # 103 There are probably not a lot of prairie voles around. So they do not meet potential mates very often. So when a prairie vole meets an unattached prairie vole of the opposite sex a special chemical is released in the brain which locks each one on to the other for ever. It is like an instant mutual obsession. Of the people I have mentioned this to, some like the idea very much because it removes the doubts, hassle and fickleness of human love. Others declare themselves appalled by this mechanical lack of choice and chance arranged marriage.

A person caught up in an obsession is enslaved by that obsession. Independent and objective judgement is lost. The obsession controls all thinking, all feeling and almost all action.

 # 104 A puppet may seem full of life and animation but every movement and every expression is controlled through the attached strings by someone else.

As we go through life we become 'puppets' to a lot of

factors that control and determine how we feel and what we do.

That independence which we believe to arise from 'free will' is often only an illusion. We are 'free' to do what we are supposed to do, just as a puppet is 'free' to jerk about as required.

This does not mean that this control is bad. It might sometimes be very good. Nor does it mean that control is bad and freedom from control is good. It might even be exactly the other way around.

Awareness of the 'possibility' of these multiple controlling influences is part of wisdom.

 # 105   Christian and Jewish upbringings are supposed to depend very heavily on 'guilt'.

There is the story of a mother who gave her son two beautiful shirts for his birthday. One shirt was red and the other shirt was blue.

Next morning the son came down for breakfast proudly wearing the blue shirt. His mother looked at his shirt and snarled: 'So what is wrong with the red shirt?'

A steady diet of guilt builds up a dependence on parents and also provides a solid base for discipline and instilling those values that are going to be of so much use to the child himself or herself, and society in general. Guilt is a powerful and efficient mechanism for education and for getting done what needs to be done. It is too easy and fashionable to condemn guilt for its neurosis-building aspect and to forget to appreciate its guidance role. The Christian conscience is a repository of guilt and guidance. The guiltless person is either unimaginative or a sociopath.

Freud, who was dealing with a very guilt-ridden sector of society (the chocolate-eating young ladies of Vienna), formalized the traditional conscience as the 'super-ego' that presides over our normal egos and pulls the puppet strings.

 # 106   When we are not controlled by guilt we are prisoners of expectation.

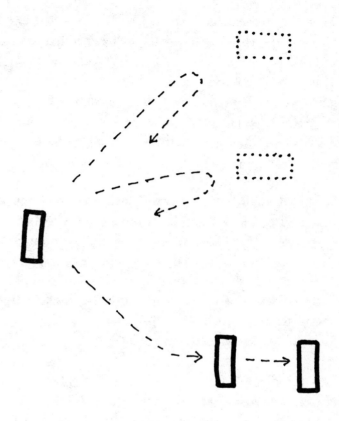

We are hostage to guilt, which guides our behaviour by a sort of electrified
fence which we dare not cross. We back away.

There are the expectations we have of ourselves.

There are the expectations that we are expected to have of ourselves. For example, that all women should marry.

There are the multiple expectations that others (parents, partners, teachers, friends, hairdressers, etc.) have of us. We have to buy the right house in the right place and own the right car in order to satisfy our consideration of these expectations.

People like bad horror movies because the bad guys are supposed to be bad and they make every effort to fulfil expectations. Real-life movies are too full of complex psychodrama in which a character does not really know whether he or she is supposed to be bad or good. We do want expectations to be clear and to be fulfilled. If the wrong actress runs off with a pizza waiter we get upset. If the right actress does so we applaud.

Expectations are somewhat like the multiple walls of a prison. When you get over the first wall you find there is another. Wives have expectations of husbands. These are formalized as duties, responsibilities, obligations and human caring. Husbands have expectations of wives. These are formalized as femininity, mothering, competence and human caring.

There are the powerful expectations which people have of themselves. These are both the source of happiness and the source of unhappiness (see *The Happiness Purpose*, Penguin 1990). Without expectations we get no further than where we are – which may be fine if that is what you prefer. It is expectations of ourselves that drive us on to

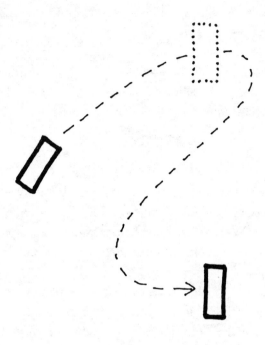

We are hostage to the expectations we have of ourselves – whether these are positive or negative. We behave to fit these expectations.

achievement and success. Most successful people have had strong expectations of themselves. At the same time, unhappiness is the gap between expectations and the talent to fulfil them.

Just as the big guy Gulliver was tethered by the hundreds of ropes of the tiny Lilliputians, so we are tethered by multiple expectations.

107 Of course, we may choose to be tethered. We may welcome the puppet strings. We may prefer 'dependence' to independence. We may like our identity, values and choices to be determined by someone outside our own skin.

We may prefer to be dependent on another person, on a parent, on a partner, on a leader or on a group. Why should we take the complex responsibility for our own ego, values and decisions? Why not have the freedom of a child who likes doing what he or she is told to do?

This is like allowing someone else into your 'skin' so that your organized identity now includes that other person.

Religion encourages this: 'not my will but God's will through me'. Some of the most saintly lives have worked that way.

108 For youngsters faced with the problems and changing values of growing up, the peer group of mates is the best source of identity. Your parents, by definition, do not

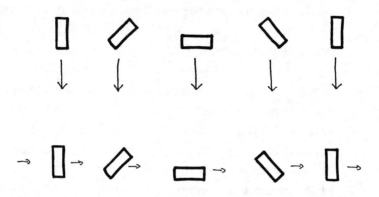

Very often we are hostage to the fashion of the moment, whether it is within a small peer group or a larger group or the world around. Fashion determines what we should value, think and do.

understand the modern world. And when they do they appear grotesque. Parents are meant to be parents, not adult teenagers. So your identity is derived from your dependence on the group or gang. There may be a leader in that group or there may be a number of trend-setters.

Values are expressed as fashion. Just as dress designers rely on a constant change of fashion in order to keep their leadership, so group leaders also need changes of fashion in order to remain leaders. They are the first into the new fashion because that automatically makes other members of the group into followers. Of course, group leaders have to judge very finely when a fashion is ripe for a change otherwise they go out on a limb and lose their leadership. Political leaders have the same problem: to lead from in front by sensing where people are heading anyway.

If the group is into celibacy then that is your choice. If the group is into sex then that is your choice. If the group is into smoking or drugs then that is your choice.

 # 109 Some species of whales go around in groups or 'pods'. Dolphins like to live together. In the animal world there are herds, packs and colonies. It is very basic and natural for some living creatures to want to be together and part of a larger group. This may be for security, for mutual assistance or just for 'company'. Why have to decide for yourself which way to migrate to lusher pastures when the herd will make the decision for you?

We cherish independent behaviour so much that we look

down on 'herd behaviour'. Why? What is wrong with being a sheep?

Wisdom is a matter of making your own choices. If you choose to get your identity from the group that is your choice.

You do not need to be permanently bound by that choice or bound by it in all matters. People who follow fashion slavishly still allow themselves moments of difference.

 # 110 A paranoid person is slave to an extra intensity of meaning. In depression nothing has a meaning and nothing has a value. In paranoia everything has a super-organized meaning.

Fanaticism is another example of a super-organized meaning and purpose. Perceptions, beliefs, ideals, values and actions are directed to the 'mission'. Identity is derived from that mission.

 # 111 Can you be a great artist or a great leader without 'passion'? Passion is a commitment of feelings, effort and everything else to some performance. A passionate opera singer and a passionate lover have much in common – including being self-centred. Much of the value of rock music comes from the apparent passion of the performers. Youth wants to feel passionate and it is nice to have someone show you how in a medium where this is more possible than in ordinary life.

An artist is a slave to his or her passion and wants it that way. A commitment that takes you over and pulls you along with it is what most people want.

Is wisdom, then, a 'spoilsport' which stands back and advises you that you are 'enslaved' by this passion? A cook who uses curry or chilli knows how to use it. You do not create a dish that is so hot that it is uneatable.

#112 The usual baggage of language means that words like hostage, slave, prisoner and puppet all have 'bad' meanings. What about being a 'positive' slave or hostage?

Some of the most worthwhile lives have been lived by people who have become willing positive hostages to the beliefs, ideals and values of religious systems. Why create your own values when better ones can be taken up?

#113 We sometimes do not realize how strongly we are culturally enslaved by 'slogans' and principles.

The banner of 'social justice' is a cover for all sorts of activity, some of which is directly contrary to social justice.

We are enslaved by the concept of 'democracy' because we have invested so much rhetoric in it and because we are too feeble to design something better. Compared to tyranny, democracy is wonderful. Compared to 'what might be', democracy is mediocre.

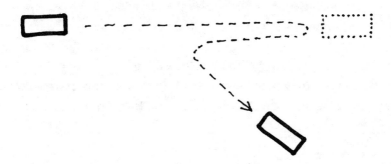

We are always completely hostage to the limited words of language. We have to use available words. Language is an encyclopedia of ignorance, which forces us to perceive and communicate in a limited way.

'Freedom' is another slogan that restricts our action. There can be no curtailment of violence on television because that would be an interference with freedom – and where would that stop (and who is to decide?)?

There is a very reasonable reluctance to tamper with these absolutes because our traditional thinking system tells us that once they are not absolute they are nothing and are gone for ever.

So our thinking is enslaved in this way. We are bullied by those who wield these traditional slogans not as banners but as weapons.

'History' is another sacred cow and so is 'culture'. Just as people are enslaved to adore a particular idol, so these 'intellectual idols' demand unconditional adoration.

It is part of wisdom to challenge this assumed reverence from time to time. And to ask what is beneath the protective banner.

 # 114 Society could not work at all unless we gave unconditional reverence to certain principles. These we believe to be the basic principles of civilized behaviour, which is contrasted with a jungle free-for-all.

Justice, caring for the less advantaged, freedom from excessive interference, are all part of those accepted principles which were at one time crystallized in the American Constitution.

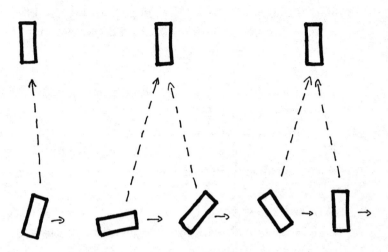

Behaviour can be guided by reverence for unchanging principles of which we are conscious at every moment.

There is a willing submission to these principles because this is an investment. To accept the principle of justice means that you hope also to get justice when you need it. To applaud law and order means that you are more likely to be a beneficiary from this than a victim of it.

Here again we see the operation of 'positive enslavement'.

The monk who chooses to follow a rigid routine in the monastery knows that this routine will give him the freedom to pray and contemplate.

Wisdom knows that the choice is not between freedom and restriction, but between either/or choices and the designed use of both.

 # 115 If you are walking along a path then the very next step is largely conditioned by where you are at the moment. So you take that next step along the path. The next step is again conditioned by where you are – and so on.

We can become trapped by continuity. We start something off and then we are trapped into continuing it.

In theory, you could turn back along the path or step off the path in an entirely new direction. In practice it is not nearly so easy. If you are halfway through cooking a particular dish, do you have complete freedom of choice? If a sculptor has committed herself to a certain shape in the use of the marble, is she really free to pursue a different shape?

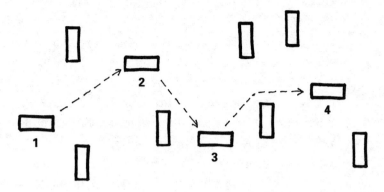

We are hostage to routine because taking the next step along a routine path is so much easier than choosing any other step.

Why am I doing this? Because I am in a certain position where the next step forward is determined by where I am.

In theory, I could cease to write this book at this moment or might change to a totally different subject like the digestion of vegetable matter by wasps. If I had done either you would not be reading this book. In this particular case I am as much trapped by the objective (and ambition) as by where I am.

There are people who, to the surprise of their friends, decide to drop out. They leave good jobs on Wall Street and go to live a simple life on a Pacific island. That is what Gauguin did, except that it was Paris and not Wall Street.

Wisdom is knowing that you have this choice. The next step does not have to be determined by where you are right now.

 # 116 In a self-organizing system like the human brain the 'patterns' are set up by the particular 'sequence' of experience. Exactly the same experiences in a different sequence would have given different concepts and perceptions.

One of the logical reasons why we need creativity is to escape from a particular sequence of experience in order to put things together in a different way.

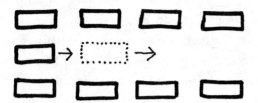

We may be hostage to circumstance. We may choose to put ourselves into circumstances where values and actions are thereafter determined by those circumstances. Sometimes we are put there against our will.

You are given a few cardboard shapes and are asked to fit them together to make a recognized geometric figure (square, rectangle, triangle, etc.). You play around with them and construct such a shape. You are given other pieces. You can fit them into the existing shape. For example, you might lengthen the rectangle. Then you are given further pieces. But these new pieces will not 'fit' in. In order to proceed you have to pull apart the shape you have in order to reassemble all the pieces into a new shape.

It is the same with life. Experiences come in. They form themselves into concepts and perceptions. New experiences can be added to these concepts and perceptions. There comes a time, however, when these new experiences do not fit well into the old arrangements. At that point we need to go back to change our fundamental concepts and perceptions. That is why creativity is necessary.

Without creativity we remain trapped within that particular sequence of experience that gave us the concept or perception.

Wisdom demands the use of creativity.

 # 117 Routines have a value. We should not too easily condemn them as boring. It is said that the great philosopher Emmanuel Kant was so regular in his routines that people used to set their watches by his appearance outside their house on his routine walk.

As with the monk who chooses the routine of the monastery, routines can give us the freedom to do other things. The routine of the assembly line enables the workers to chat about other matters.

People go on holiday to escape from their usual day-to-day routine. As soon as they get to the holiday destination they set up another routine: breakfast, pool, lunch, beach, drinks, dinner at a new restaurant.

Cruise ships are ever-growing in popularity because of the routines. Everything is laid out. You do not have the hassle of seeking out a cute new restaurant every evening.

Though very few people will admit it, most people are bullied by opportunity. There are so many opportunities that people get confused and find it difficult to make decisions. If you choose this, it means giving up this and this. Young people who would happily marry if they remained in their villages go to the big city and are confused by the opportunities.

If you can do everything then how do you choose what to do? A handicapped person may find great satisfaction in doing something simple because the range of options has been so narrowed.

How does wisdom look on routine? In the first place, wisdom acknowledges the value of routine and refuses to condemn routine just because it is routine. In the second place, wisdom appreciates when routine is useful and when it is restrictive. Wisdom may also be involved in changing and redesigning routines.

Above all, wisdom realizes that we may indeed be trapped by routines. Once we realize this we can accept it as what we want (and valuable), or seek to escape. Escape is not automatically a value.

 # 118 It is possible to be a hostage to your own self-image or style. Your sense of identity is so closely tied in to your sense of style that you dare not change it. Nor would you know what to do.

As I have mentioned earlier in this book it is said that the great British prime minister, Lady Thatcher, had such a strong sense of style that in making a decision it was enough for her to say to herself: 'What would Mrs Thatcher do here?'

Self-image and style are closely tied up with expectations. A painter with a highly recognizable style is trapped by that style. A playwright with a recognizable style is trapped by that style. To some extent, I am trapped by the expectation that I should always say new things.

The student who is good at mathematics at school is trapped by that excellence. The student goes on to do mathematics at university and may end up teaching mathematics. Or the student is advised to take up a subject like engineering, which requires maths ability. Yet that student might have been far happier as a cook running a restaurant. We can indeed be trapped by our talents and what we, and others, expect us to do with those talents.

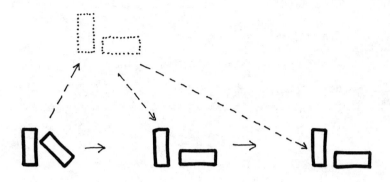

We may be hostage to our own personal self-images. We act out the role which we have designed for ourselves. We cannot think of stepping outside that role.

 # 119 So what is the overall wisdom response to 'hostage, slave, prisoner and puppet'?

Awareness

As in so many places, the starting-point for wisdom is awareness. These things can happen. We can be a hostage to emotions and expectations. We can be enslaved by slogans and routines. We can be trapped by excellence. In any situation we need to give some thought to these aspects. 'Why are we doing this?'

No Condemnation

It is only too easy to condemn almost all the types of enslavement mentioned in this chapter. Surely initiative is better than routine? Surely personal choice is better than group choice? Surely we should not act just to fulfil the expectations of others? These would be traditional simplistic judgements. There are times when routines are excellent. There are times when enslavement by positive ideals is of great value. We need to look at each situation in its own right. We must refuse to be enslaved by the baggage of language and fashionable simple judgements.

Shrug

If someone insults you, you are not insulted if you choose not to be insulted. The 'shrug' may be difficult at first but it is very powerful. The shrug frees you from being hostage to your own emotions and to others who can trigger those emotions. The shrug is a deliberate action which you have to practise so that when you really need it you know how to do it (see *The Happiness Purpose,*

Penguin 1990). The shrug is how we detach ourselves from the puppet strings of expectations: 'If people are disappointed that is their problem.'

Pause

The 'pause' is how we avoid the immediate cliché response or action. We pause to consider what is driving us. We pause to consider alternative perceptions. We pause to consider alternative courses of action. There is no need to think quickly. Pause and think slowly instead. Pause and reflection go together.

Choice

In the end there is choice. Do I want to follow this routine or not? Do I want to act according to my style on this occasion? Do I want to go along with the group-think? Treat it as a choice which may go either way.

I, We and Identity

 # 120   What sign of the Zodiac are you? What is your Chinese astrological sign? If a Chinese girl has the combined signs of 'tiger' and 'fire' her birthday is kept secret, for otherwise no one would marry her. It is said that the birth rates in Chinese communities vary considerably according to whether it is a good or bad sign to be born under.

Some people look 'under their stars' for fun. Others take it quite seriously.

How do we know who we are? The Zodiac signs provide neat little boxes. We are placed in a box according to our birth date. There is no subjective judgement about it. Then we read out from that box who we are.

How else can we tell who we are? We suspect that our own assessment will be biased and incomplete. We suspect that our friends will not tell us the truth. We may prefer to pay an expensive psychiatrist to tell us.

 # 121   In the days of the Cold War there were major spy scandals from time to time. I was always amazed at how little money spies were paid for very dangerous assignments that could cost them their careers and even their lives (as

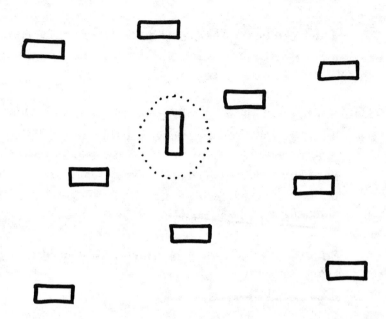

Everyone wants to feel special, unique and important in some way.

with the Rosenbergs). Why would anyone want to take such risks?

There can be the ideological drive. There can be entrapment, where one small step leads to another and through blackmail someone becomes a reluctant spy.

In some cases I believe the driving force is the feeling of 'being special'. You are sitting in a restaurant with lots of people around you. Not one of them knows that you are a spy. You feel very special and different from everyone else in that restaurant. Your friends think they know you. But you are more special than they think.

So being a spy is a powerful definition of your identity.

 # 122 In a way, all 'missions' give a sense of identity. With terrorist groups there is both the sense of 'mission' and also the sense of identity derived from the group identity.

In the old days IBM had such a very strong corporate culture that people who worked for IBM felt themselves to be IBM-ers. They were proud to belong to that group. When IBM workers were asked if they would like to join unions they usually declined. Who needed to belong to a union if you already belonged to IBM?

Motor cycle gangs have a notorious sense of identity and pitched battles between rival gangs have left people dead.

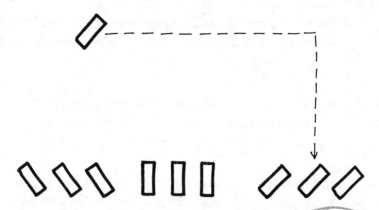

Where do I belong? In which group do I belong through birth, race, age, etc.? In which group do I belong through feelings and values?

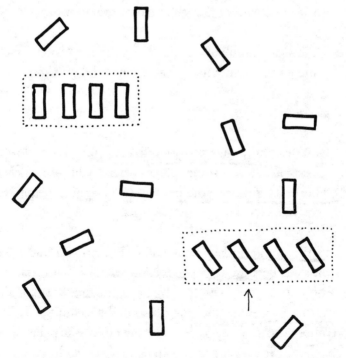

You can get your sense of identity by belonging to a group or gang of like-minded people.

The Los Angeles street gangs have their own sense of identity and drive-by shootings are an unpleasant expression of that identity.

Gangs give people a sense of identity through belonging. They not only have their own puny identities but there is now the larger, more powerful identity of the gang.

It is interesting that in some countries, like Latin America and China, the family is itself a 'gang' with a strong sense of identity. In other countries families are regarded as no more than a necessary part of growing up. Family members might always be ready to help another family member who was in trouble, but otherwise they would rather be further apart than closer together.

I knew one family in the USA who spent $900,000 a year suing each other. That is one form of relationship.

———

 # 123 Families and gangs provide identity, purpose and a base. There is always some place where you are accepted. There are always some people who might be expected to help you.

In the outer world people will only help you out of compassion, because they like you or because they need something from you. With the gang and the family you get help automatically without having to be liked too much. It is a mutual insurance scheme like any other mutual insurance scheme. You all agree to help each other. Help is no longer based on individual assessment at any one moment.

The 'values' involved in belonging have already been considered in a previous chapter. Here we are concerned with the sense of 'identity'.

———

 # 124 Imagine yourself at a football match where your favourite team is playing. Would you ever consider shouting support for the other team? It would be unthinkable. You would be tearing your own identity apart.

We define our group identity as much by what we dislike as by what we like. You feel obliged to dislike the other group in order to reaffirm the boundaries of your own group. You seek to show your fervent support by insulting and even attacking the supporters of the other football team.

Ethnic hatred of another group is what defines the specialness and superiority of your own group. Hate gives a permanent mission.

The group that is the subject of the hatred gets an even stronger sense of identity. The very strong sense of identity of the Jewish community comes from centuries of persecution. The early Christian communities were also advantaged by being persecuted from time to time.

 # 125 People seek to be acceptable in clubs and groups. The expression 'he is one of us' occurs in several languages and means acceptance in the group.

In India the caste system defines groups in a rigid way. In Japan people whose ancestors were tanners several centuries ago are still defined by that grouping. Tanners lived together in villages rendered smelly by their work. So no

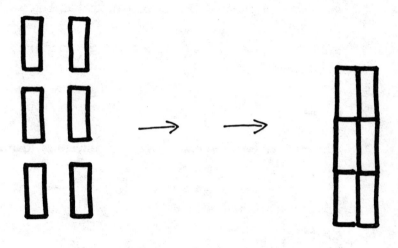

A group is not a collection of individuals but acquires a special 'group' identity that is more than the sum of its parts.

one wanted to marry a tanner. Today there are special detective agencies which you employ to check whether your son or daughter is going to marry one of these people. Foreigners in Japan are still regarded as foreigners even if they have lived there for several generations (as some Koreans have).

 # 126 The Japanese seem to have a different concept of identity from the Western one. In the West there is a single ego which integrates the person throughout the day. At the office, at home and at a reception.

In Japan, the group culture is so much stronger than the ego culture that there sometimes seems to be a totally different person on different occasions. During the day there is the 'business' man. In the evening there is the 'Japanese businessman', who goes to his girlie clubs and drinks far too much. In the later evening there is the 'family' man, who goes home and is a dutiful husband and gets bullied by his docile wife.

There is more sense of fitting and integrating into the group rather than expressing an individual ego all the time. Egos are regarded as rather crude and pushy. Having a strong ego is not unlike having bad breath. No one wants to get too close to you.

 # 127 Philosophy has always had a big problem with consciousness. We can see a machine working but we know that the machine does not have a consciousness of its own

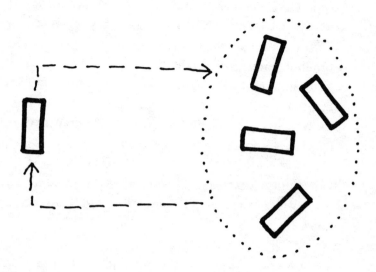

Our consciousness of self is our awareness of the underlying link between our different moods, activities and thoughts.

working. 'Consciousness' is the typical sort of philo-sophical non-problem, like the apparent argument be-tween free will and determinism. We set things up in such a way that we cannot be satisfied by any answer.

Imagine there is a bright light behind you at all times. Your shadow is continually thrown on the white wall in front of you. You become aware of your shape and your movements. Through this external shadow device you develop a 'consciousness' of yourself.

If we put a bright light behind the machine and gave it some way of observing its shadow, would that machine be conscious?

We are conscious of where our limbs are because there are sensors in the muscle which tell us which muscles are being used. In a large brewery I visited recently, in Malta, a highly automated system showed on a central computer screen the state of every fluid valve in the system. That computer screen was the 'consciousness' of the system.

As an organizing boundary for our consciousness of 'self' we find it convenient to choose the limits of our own skin. When we derive our sense of identity from the group, that 'skin' is enlarged to include the group as well.

———

 # 128 There may be a dependence on a group for identity or there may be a dependence on one other person. That other person provides the evaluation of behaviour. You seek that other person's approval. That other person pro-vides direction and action choices. That other person sets the values and perceptions. You cannot make your own mistakes. Uncertainties and confusions are lessened. You just want to follow or to 'flow' with the action.

With a group, not only do you depend on the whole group for identity but your personal identity also depends on your accepted position in the group. The way the other members of the group treat you defines your personal identity. Italian groups are excellent at assigning different roles and positions to all group members.

 # 129 In one of its aspects love is a form of dependence. We want 'attention' and 'approval' from that other person. If it is not forthcoming or is cut off we feel worthless enough to commit suicide.

We rarely have the sense of perspective to treat love as we might treat a bout of influenza – something that comes and goes. It is not a matter of our 'ego' being involved with another 'ego'. Instead, our ego exists through its dependence on another ego. It is sometimes said that you have to be slightly neurotic to be truly in love.

Is love selfish because it demands and expects? Is love selfless because it wants to give? But is that giving no more than an investment in getting?

 # 130 It could be argued that all our actions are 'selfish'. Even the most selfless behaviour of a saint could be seen to be selfish for a number of reasons:

1. It makes that person 'feel good' to be selfless and to help others. There is a sense of mission, fulfilment, accomplishment and virtue.

2. It makes that person feel good to know that he or she is pleasing God and following God's will.

3. It makes that person feel good to know that a good example has been given to others who might also set about helping the less fortunate.

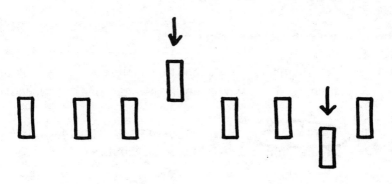

In a club or class, if you seek to rise above the average ability you are pushed back. If you fall below the average level you are pushed out.

So we have the conundrum: is it selfish to be selfless when being selfless is what you want to do most of all?

 # 131 Our identity can be defined to ourselves by our actions and choices as much as by group labels or personal introspection.

Actions express values, personality and capability. Actions can give that success which also identifies us.

There are also times when action can be a way of escaping from having to think about oneself. Instead of reflection and introspection you busy yourself with endless action. Distraction is like a train that is always moving and never has to get anywhere.

 # 132 Since Freud there has been a well-established notion that feelings should be expressed. If they are repressed this is supposed to lead to stomach ulcers and neurosis and lots of other bad things.

The expression of feelings is obviously beneficial because otherwise how are other people going to know what you feel? Also, if you express your feelings all the time, then no one takes them very seriously on any one occasion. Because Mediterranean people are always expressing their feelings, an apparently violent argument means far less than it would in England. People who seem the most violent of enemies are seen drinking together as friends two hours later. The theatre of emotions is seen as such.

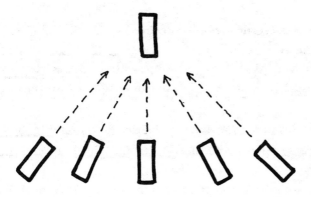

You can get a sense of identity through attention and fame but you then become very dependent upon this for your identity.

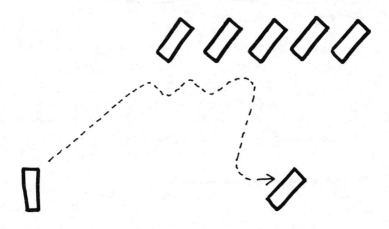

Identity can also be obtained through absorbing the corporate culture around you.

'I love you for ever or until next Monday,' is both sincere and practical.

There does come a point, however, where self-expression becomes very selfish indeed. You need to express yourself, so you 'dump' on anyone around. You need to be 'assertive', so other people's sensitivities are unimportant.

Freud started the movement that declared that inhibitions were 'bad'. Does this imply that lack of inhibitions is good?

Inhibitions are the lubrication of civilization. Without inhibitions you do not care what you do. You do not care if you upset someone. You do not care if you shirk your responsibilities. You do not care if you let people down.

Wisdom suggests that in the matter of 'inhibitions' we have a classic 'salt curve' or 'Laffer curve'.

– no inhibitions is bad

– some inhibitions is good

– too much inhibitions is bad.

The 'me' cult of self-expression only works if the bulk of what is expressed is constructive.

133   Identity can be established through self-conscious style. The one thing Oscar Wilde was producing throughout his life was 'himself'.

The traditional post-Freudian approach has been to dig ever deeper in an attempt to discover the 'true self'.

But maybe when you dig deeper you discover more and more garbage. This 'digging' for the truth is an arbitrary model derived from the Gang of Three.

Maybe we should be in the 'design' business rather than the 'excavation' business. Maybe we should be designing our own style or the 'mask' behind which we want to face the world.

Maybe the ego and identity are to be designed and constructed through continued effort. They are not there to begin with, they need not be borrowed and they are not going to be discovered.

It is part of wisdom to realize this possibility.

How do you want to be? Design it and do it.

 # 134 There are times when we seek to establish our identity with titles, status and power.

These are devices that ensure that people give us respect. In New York I have sometimes been surprised to find myself having lunch with someone who has assumed a title in order to get a better table reservation.

Sometimes these external definitions of identity give a person enough confidence to develop a true identity. Sometimes they have exactly the opposite effect and these artificial props prevent the development of any other identity. Both are possible.

Boys who go to Eton (a leading school in England) acquire a special sort of confidence that they are an élite. That confidence is valuable if it becomes the base for developing

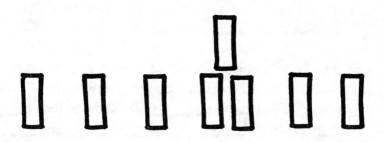

We acquire status within a group when enough members of the group are willing to support that status.

skills and useful qualities. It is dangerous and inhibiting if it is seen as a sufficient qualification in itself.

 # 135 The world may not be as full of 'heroes' as it once seemed to be. Today's heroes are stars from the world of entertainment and sport. As role models they may have little to offer because skill in a particular field is not translatable into general lifestyle. In many cases the lifestyle itself is not specially heroic.

So 'comparison identity' is difficult. It can still be directed at parent figures, brothers or sisters. Why can't I be like that?

The setting of expectations and ambitions for oneself becomes a form of comparison identity. You then compare yourself with that image or ideal. This image can lead you forward. It can also create doubts. At times it can generate despair. How can I ever be like that?

 # 136 In a book (*Tactics*, Collins 1985) that was based on interviews with successful people, there was one thing that stood out. Almost all the successful people had had a strong sense of 'the expectation of success'. When things were bad and there was a downturn of fortune they did not despair. They regarded every downturn as merely another step towards the goal.

This strong sense of perspective is a key factor in wisdom.

When you are depressed you believe that you are now

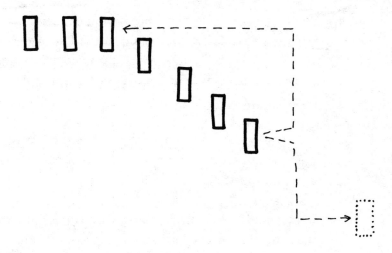

When we are depressed we believe that we see the true reality and regard
our normal state as an illusion.

being realistic and that the dreams you had at other times are no more than dreams. You are ready to give up. The depressed state of mind is seen as the 'realistic' state of mind. The depressed state of mind is the truly abnormal state of mind. Your dreams are still as valid as they were before. Depression is like feeling seasick. Even the thought of food nauseates you. The seasickness passes and food tastes great again.

How do you know if your dreams are realistic? How do you know if you are ever going to attain them? Can every politician become prime minister?

A scientist holds a hypothesis and works with it. There is no guarantee that this hypothesis is going to work out. It is something to be going forward with. When accumulating evidence suggests that the hypothesis is not going to work the scientist sets about designing a new hypothesis.

It is the same with dreams. Stay with them until accumulating evidence suggests they are not going to work. Then change them – or stay with them if they still keep you happy. That is wisdom. Being realistic is often part of wisdom but not always.

137   A plant is not fully grown until it is fully grown. Imagine a plant that went on growing and developing until it died. An identity is not a roll of film that you take to be developed. The developed film then reveals 'what is' and what will be for ever. An identity is like the ever-growing

plant. The potential is there and the general form is there. The leaves and the branches make up the plant even as habits, dreams, talents and achievements make up identity.

Contribute

 # 138   Right now I want to have fun. Later on there will be heavy and serious things to be done. Now I want to celebrate existence and being alive. Anyway, I am growing up and developing and finding out what the world is all about and what I am all about. I am also studying and taking my exams.

I did not ask to be born. I exist. The world, the government or someone owes me a living. Those who have should look after those who do not have. It is not my fault that I am not talented and have not had the right chances.

Who wants to live a boring life doing only those things that you are supposed to do? I want to live now and not save everything for the future. What is the point of striving harder and harder if you do not enjoy it?

It is possible to put forward a framework of reasons and values to justify almost any choice of lifestyle. If you choose your perceptions, choose your values and choose your information, you can defend almost any point of view. Who is to say which set of values is the better one? There are families in which one child has been ambitious and has worked hard and has earned the material support for a 'rich' life. Another child has been content to live a simpler life without ambition.

PASSIVE

ACTIVE

Some people are active and some people prefer to be passive.

Each person has to decide for himself or herself the life values and lifestyle that he or she wants. In making this choice there are two related points:

1. That you are conscious that the choice is being made

2. That the background for a fair choice is there.

Does the choice have to be a conscious 'sit down and decide' choice or can it be a 'drift choice', where something gradually becomes apparent? There is a variety of ways of making choices.

Even when the choice has been made, it may be impossible to implement that choice because of the 'edge effect': the first steps may be impossible to take.

 # 139 We can calculate how much of our lives we spend asleep. It is not so easy to calculate how much of our life is spent in 'time filling'. There is nothing you feel like doing at this moment so you 'exist' until the next event or until your energy returns. If you were a lion you would probably go to sleep. As a human you watch television instead. Is there anything wrong with this? Is there anything wrong with eating porridge? Porridge is an excellent food but you may not want porridge at every meal. Porridge is an excellent food but you may sometimes want a hamburger or lobster. There does not have to be something 'wrong' with porridge to suggest that you may enjoy other choices as well.

What if you are so content with porridge that you never want to try anything else? What if you are not even aware that there is anything else? What if you cannot afford

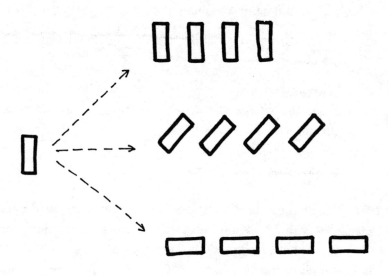

There is always a choice of lifestyles. You can go with the flow, time-fill, do things or drift along.

anything else? You make your choice or you have your choices forced upon you. You may choose to be content with porridge or you may choose to try to work towards something different. 'To try' is never a guarantee of success. But 'not to try' is a guarantee of failure.

Wisdom is a matter of awareness and choice. Choice of values and choice of the direction in which to make some effort.

 # 140 When there is nothing particular you want to do then watching TV is considerably better than sitting in a chair and doing nothing. Once you are watching TV it is considerably easier to go on watching rather than to start something else.

In the USA children spend more time watching TV than at school. Is this bad? Not at all. Are there other things that might have been more worth while? Probably.

How do we get to do those things that we will enjoy once we have started to do them? How do you know you are going to enjoy stamp collecting until after you have built up a small collection?

There is investment and there is risk. People invest in a business because they know that there is a money reward in a successful business. People invest in a business because they believe that the particular business idea has a good chance of success. They are willing to take the risk because of the potential reward.

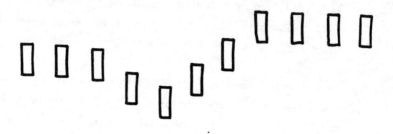

Investment means putting in some time and energy, which may seem negative at the moment, in order to get more back later – spending hours learning to play a musical instrument so that your life is enriched later.

But how do you invest time and effort in something new when the reward is not as defined as in the business example? You may see your friends doing something and decide that you ought to try. You may set yourself the principle of trying something new from time to time.

Learning to ride a bicycle is not easy, not fun and not a good way of getting anywhere. The learning period is hard work. But when you have learned how to ride a bicycle you enjoy it and get to places faster. You may need to apply the 'bicycle' model to other activities.

 # 141 A cow in a field is content and doing what the peer group all around is doing. Who is to say that the cow is less happy than the racehorse which is trained hard and pushed to the limit by its jockey?

If you had a good singing voice would you want to sing? An Australian girl was discovered as a potential opera singer when she was heard singing after a barbecue. So should one sing after barbecues in the hope of being discovered – like attractive girls going to be waitresses in Los Angeles drug stores because some famous actresses were discovered in this way? Claudia Schiffer, the super-model, was discovered in a discothèque. You sing because you enjoy singing. If you do get discovered that is a bonus. You can also choose to sing in order to get discovered. That is simply another option.

 # 142 Some people contribute and some people are passive.

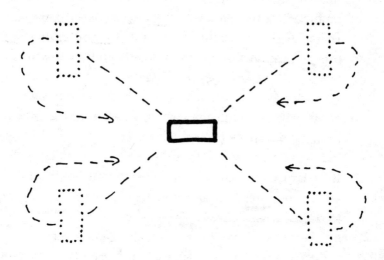

Boredom means that you contribute nothing to the world, but demand that the world amuse you. If you do not open an interest then that interest is blind.

Being passive may be a choice based on a full experience of contributing and not contributing. Being passive may be based on the choice of 'laziness' as a low-hassle state. Being passive may also be based on lack of experience of the joy of contributing. How do you know you would not like figs if you have never tasted them?

If you are cold and hungry it is nice to feel warm. It is even nicer to have some food as well.

Boredom is an unpleasant state. If you could both get rid of the boredom and also have something enjoyable to do, then you have two values. Taking an aspirin for a headache only has one value: getting rid of the headache.

Boredom is one of the most powerful emotions though few psychologists would classify it as such. Contribution can get rid of the boredom and give the plus of involvement and achievement. To treat boredom only with further distraction is more like the aspirin. The headache goes away only while the aspirin is working. You may need stronger and stronger aspirin just as you may come to need stronger and stronger distraction if that is your only cure for boredom.

 # 143 There is usually a chemical component to severe depression and it is not just a reaction to the world around. In other types of depression there may be some external cause.

If everything depends on the relationship and ambition of the moment, then when this fails there is nothing worth doing.

Companies that make consumer products usually have 'product champions'. These are people who are specifically assigned to look after a new product. Without such a product champion, when a new product faltered or hit a bad patch things got worse and worse. People lost faith in the product, resources were withdrawn and the critics chorused 'we told you so'. It was the role of the product champion to see new products through these 'downs': to put energy into the product, to get things back on track and to fight for resources.

Who is the 'product champion' when things are down for a person? There are parents, friends, counsellors and psychiatrists. There is also the framework of religious faith. To these can be added the continuity of contribution. Contribution has its own momentum. There is something to be done so you keep going. Contribution means that you can look beyond the despair of the moment. The time frame is larger.

 # 144 The choice is between being passive and contributing. You can contribute to yourself, to those around you or to the world at large.

Being passive is like being a cork floating in a stream. You go wherever the stream takes you. Contributing is like being in a canoe on the stream. You can go where you want or let the stream take you. You can go through white-water rapids because you have control. The cork can also go through the rapids but only because it cannot be damaged.

There is a joy in passivity. There is a joy in surrendering to 'what will be'. For some people there is a surrender to 'fate' or an offer of submission to 'God's will'.

There is also a lot of anxiety and uncertainty in passivity. You are at the mercy of everyone, including yourself.

Do you go with the flow of nature or stand back from time to time to appreciate nature? Do trees appreciate each other?

As so often, the choice is not between being passive and being active. The first choice is between having the choice and having no choice. The second choice is to determine the mix of passivity and activity that you want. This may vary from time to time and at different stages in life.

 # 145 The world is interesting because you choose to make it interesting. There is a need to contribute. There is a need

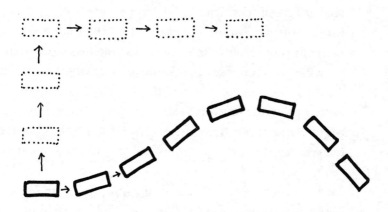

You can choose to go with the flow of events or to design your own steps and your own future.

to contribute to yourself in terms of investment of time and effort. If you choose to become an expert on cockroaches then cockroaches become interesting. If you invest time and effort in wine-tasting then wine is more interesting. If you follow in detail the exploits of your soccer team then their games become more interesting.

If you sit back and wait for 'interesting' things to happen to you, you might be limited to wild-life programmes on television.

Bird-watchers go and sit in uncomfortable places for hours when more sensible people would be watching a sport or television. But the bird-watchers have invested time and effort in understanding the patterns and subtleties of bird behaviour and are rewarded as a result.

Whenever we invest in interest we are forming 'tentacles' in the mind. These tentacles are now available to reach out and make interesting things which others would not even have noticed. These 'tentacles' are like free radicals waiting to combine with experience. They are the sensitization of different possible pathways in the brain. The more you invest in interest the more the world will become interesting.

 # 146 There is a joy in achievement. There is a joy in making things happen. I imagine that is why most gardeners garden. There is something you are doing. There is something you have done. There is something you plan to do. You can stand back and see the difference you have made to the world.

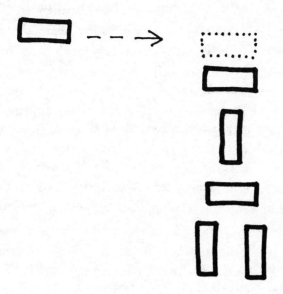

There is joy in achievement, just as a child enjoys putting yet another block on to the tower. There is something there that was not there before.

You make music. You affect the world. You affect other people. Would you make music if there was no one to listen? Yes. Achievement is what you do to yourself, not what you do to others.

 # 147   Some people have such a strong drive to contribute that they need a mission or purpose. There is a need for some direction in which to move instead of the alternative of apparently aimless drifting from day to day. Such people become missionaries, terrorists and explorers, or join protest groups.

If you have a car you may want to drive somewhere. Others may be content just to drive round and round the block to show off the car and to enjoy the sensation of driving. Does having a car mean you have a destination?

Is this strong need to contribute an innate quality or can it be acquired? It does not have to be one or the other. People often find out for themselves the joy of contributing. Others have always known it.

It is true that having an organizing framework to life (a mission) is not exactly the same as the joy of achievement. You can have a mission but never succeed in making anything happen. You can also achieve a great deal without some overriding mission. The point is that both are the opposite of passivity. An orange is not the same as an apple but both are different from a banana.

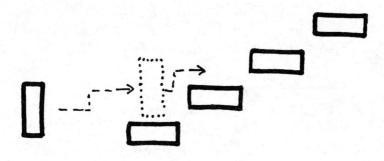

Progress means being willing to climb the steps one by one and not expecting it all to happen at once.

 # 148 In Venezuela in the jungle regions there is a story that one day when you are wandering through the jungle you will find a 'magic' tree. If you eat of the fruit of this tree then you will take control of your life and be able to do anything.

One day, in an outlying area, there was a course for teachers to train them in my CoRT thinking lessons (which are now required by law in Venezuela). I was told that at the end of the course the teachers told the instructor that they had now found the 'magic' fruit. They felt that they could now take control of their lives.

Control is a wonderful feeling when you have been out of control. To be able to make decisions and choices and to set up initiatives is very appealing. We might think of 'control' as indicating rules, regulations and strictures, but that is only one aspect of control. Imagine you are careering down the hill in a car where the brakes have gone and the steering-wheel no longer connects with the wheels. Would you not appreciate some control? You need to distinguish between the control others might exert over you and your control of your own life.

If you do not design your own life then someone else will do it for you. That 'someone' might be a person, a group or circumstances.

149 Wisdom has too often been pictured as passive, contemplative and reflective. There is the wise old person who sits and observes the world. If asked, this person will seek to pass on the accumulated wisdom of a lifetime.

There is no reason why wisdom should not be active and contribute.

Wisdom is not only a matter of adjusting to a difficult world, but also a contribution to improving that world.

 # 150   The symbol of the Positive Revolution (see *Handbook for the Positive Revolution*, Penguin 1992) is the hand. The thumb indicates 'effectiveness', because without effectiveness everything remains a dream. The index finger points the way 'forward' in the sense of constructive thinking. The middle finger indicates 'human values', which provide the justification and purpose for all that is intended. The ring finger represents 'self-improvement'. The little finger indicates 'contribution'. Even when the contribution is tiny it eventually builds up into something significant.

 # 151   Wisdom is more like gardening than just taking an excellent photograph of the garden.

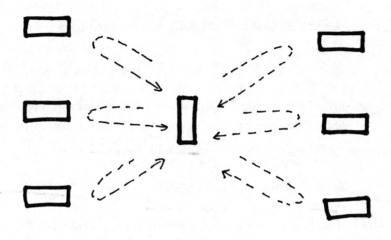

Some people believe the world owes them everything and that they do not have to contribute beyond breathing and eating.

The Beach and the Road

 # 152 You can walk anywhere on the beach. You do not have to walk. You can sit and lie and watch the waves come in. There is no road. But the beach is limited.

A road heads in a certain direction. You are confined to the road. Your choices are limited. You can choose the direction. You can choose the combination of roads. But the road restricts full freedom of movement.

 # 153 Is wisdom like a suntan, like scrambling eggs, like a photographer's flashbulb or like an aspirin?

We make some effort to acquire a suntan. For a while it is there and looks wonderful. Then it wears off. It is a memory. You know you did have that tan once upon a time. So the points made in this book may stay with you for a while. And then, like the suntan, they fade from your mind.

Scrambling eggs is a skill. It is not difficult to scramble eggs. But it is difficult to scramble eggs really well. You may learn the ways of wisdom. You may use wisdom adequately or very well. The skill remains with you – but you have to choose to use that skill. Unlike the suntan it is not there all the time.

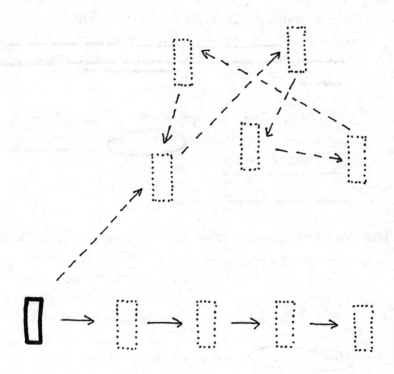

You follow along a road; the direction of movement is set out before you.
On a beach you can move in any direction.

The photographer's flashbulb is used when ordinary light is not good enough for illumination. You may choose to use wisdom when ordinary thinking seems not to be good enough. How often you use the illuminating power of wisdom will depend on your assessment of the current lighting.

An aspirin is only of value when you have a headache. You may regard wisdom as therapeutic – only to be used when there is a real problem.

 # 154 A painter does not paint with her fingers, in the air with no brush, no canvas and no colours. The full freedom of painting is not too seriously restricted by the need to apply colour to the canvas with a brush. These are specific tools which make possible the expression of the artist's vision.

How structured do we have to be in the use of wisdom?

There are people who have known what they want to do with their lives from the age of ten. There are others who go through university and still wonder what they are going to do. There are others who are content to drift about, taking each direction and each opportunity as it arises.

Can you get to a destination if you do not know where you are going? The simple answer is that you cannot. So you ought to know where you want to go. The detailed plan may not be so important as the destination.

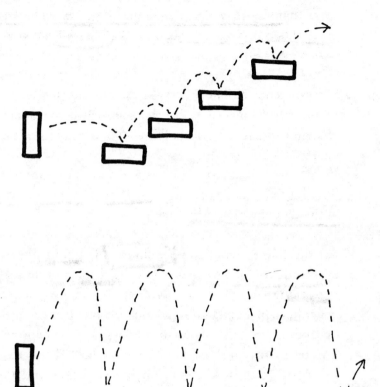

Without a road and without a structure it is much more difficult to get anywhere. The energy you put into a situation may be wasted and you are back where you started.

The more complex answer is that you can get to a destination even without knowing where you wanted to go. You simply choose to make your destination the place where you happen to have arrived. This is a *post hoc* destination.

Detailed plans give purpose, values, decisiveness and a basis for choice. There is a way of monitoring achievement. Where necessary the plan can be made flexible or changed. There is a reason for every next step.

Plans, however, restrict choices and values to ones which were set down some time ago. Plans freeze the plan-maker at the date the plans were made.

An alternative to a plan is 'evolution'. Let influences and events mould the next steps. Take advantage of all that is happening. You may end up doing something you could never have planned to do. I set out as a medical doctor but became interested in human thinking and perception as a result of my work in the more complicated systems of the body (glands, kidneys, lungs, circulation and their interaction).

Another alternative is to plan to get yourself into the best position to move in any direction that takes your fancy. Just as an athlete works towards being fit and healthy with high stamina, so you plan to develop your skills and abilities to their fullest (including wisdom). Many major corporations have given up long-term planning because in an uncertain world it is almost impossible to tell what is going to happen. So they concentrate on being efficient, fit and lean, and then wait to see in which direction to move.

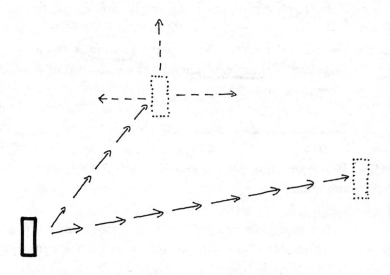

You may wish to reach a certain destination or you may wish to reach a point from which there is a choice of many destinations.

Another alternative is to decide that the hand that chance and circumstance have dealt to you is the hand you are going to play as well as you possibly can.

Another alternative is to make mini-plans which just take you a short way ahead. Then you make another mini-plan, and so on.

 # 155 If at every moment you take the most sensible step, is this not enough?

A person falls over a cliff and lands on a narrow ledge. The sensible thing is to lie still to avoid the danger of falling over the edge. But lying still will not get you rescued. Doing the most sensible thing at every step may not be a sufficient strategy. What is the most sensible step? 'Sensible' is in relation to the immediate situation, the values, the possible consequences and the overall plan. If everyone in the gang is being tattooed then that may seem the most sensible step at that moment in time. Within a large framework it may not be so sensible.

Even when there is no specific overall plan, it is the role of wisdom always to consider the 'broader picture'. Does this mean that there is no risk, no adventure and no fun? Yes, it does. So why would anyone want to be wise and bored? Because wisdom chooses adventure and fun as value choices just as an explorer makes a value choice when setting off on an expedition. You can choose to expose yourself to adventure just as you choose to go to a restaurant to expose yourself to the menu. You can choose to go gambling. The difference is that all these are now your choices.

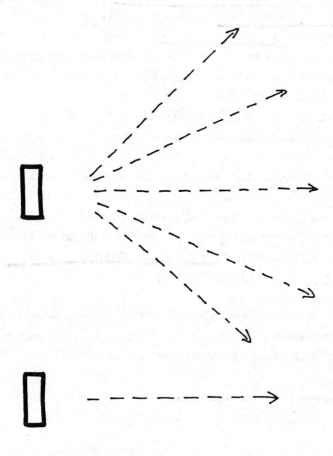

It is the purpose of wisdom always to consider the broader picture. This applies both when there is no overall plan and also when there is. The plan may need changing.

Some people do not like the burden of choice. Choice may mean rejecting something you like. Choice may mean making a mistake you will later regret. Choice may mean satisfying someone else's expectations. If some random decision-maker decided what you were going to do then that might make life easier.

It should be easiest to decide when the choices are very nearly equal. You cannot then go wrong because whatever you choose will be worth while. You might even consider tossing a coin. In practice these are often the most difficult choices, because choosing any one alternative now means giving up an almost equally attractive alternative. At this point it is best to focus not on the benefits and values but on the deficiencies: 'I would be inclined not to choose that alternative because . . .'

Young women are often advised by their magazines to focus on the negative aspects of a boyfriend who has just left. That way they are told they will miss him less.

 # 156   Where is the place for ambition? Do we become hostages to our ambitions or are ambitions the 'tractor' that pulls us forward and out of the mud?

Ambitions are contracts for future values. Your ambition might be to be a great writer. Someone else's ambition might be to have the most fun possible. Someone else's ambition might be to have a caring husband and four children. Someone else's ambition might be to drop out and simplify life.

If you want food you go to the supermarket and buy it, or you grow it or you beg for it (as young Buddhist men have to do for a while). Ambitions are the purchasing effort you make to get to your values.

Your ambition might be to have a 'peaceful unambitious life'. It is surprising how much real effort that ambition could take.

When you find making a decision difficult you may seek to avoid that difficulty by making no decision. In fact that itself is the decision. The decision to 'do nothing' is a definite decision, which will have its own consequences just as any other choice would have had consequences. 'No decision' is a valid choice provided you know that is your choice. So having 'no ambition' is itself an ambition.

 # 157 There are followers and there are leaders. There are loners and there are team members. Can you choose what to be? Is it all determined for you by some psychological profile?

Eventually, you will learn from your desires, your values and your experiences. You should never 'rule yourself out' of a possibility. People who have never thought of themselves as leaders suddenly find they are good at it and enjoy it. Lack of confidence and lack of opportunity to try something out restrict our notions of what we can and cannot do. Seek ways of trying things out.

 # 158 Some people join the army not because they want to fight but because they like the structure and discipline. You make the single decision to join and thereafter you are carried along on the values, routines and requirements that are in place.

There is nothing wrong with routines except the feeling that you cannot change them or escape from them.

Some of the wisest people set up routines.

If you had to wait until you felt inspired before sitting down to write you would achieve very little. If you set up a writing regime which you stick to firmly, then you will achieve a lot. There are times when your writing will feel less than inspired. That feeling may indeed be justified.

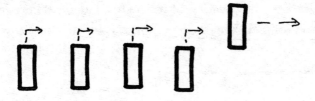

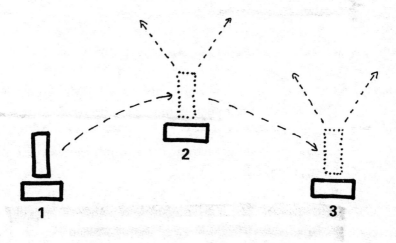

There are those who want to find direction by being led. There are those who want to lead. And there are the loners who simply want to pursue an individual direction.

Routines mean that you do not have to think about the next step, so you are freed to use your thinking on other matters. Routines can be liberating.

Over time, however, you will get a lot done. You can always drop or redo the less inspired pieces.

 # 159 'Freedom', like air, is only of value when you do not have it. If you told most people that they were suddenly free to do anything they wanted the responses would be very disappointing – unless they had always had in mind some ambition. Freedom to sit on the beach instead of working is nice as a change but as a permanent condition is probably more boring than working. Freedom to buy any excitement you want soon leads to saturation. Freedom to travel is only enjoyable if you already have an interest in other places and cultures.

If you have a can of petrol, what do you do with it? To get any value from it you need to put it into a car. To get any value from 'freedom' you need to put it into a structure of ambition or interest.

 # 160 There are always reasons and excuses why something cannot be done. Which comes first: the need to have an excuse or a genuine reason? Too often the person with a reluctance to do something casts around for a reason to support that reluctance.

Wisdom should acknowledge the validity of the reluctance in itself while rejecting the excuse. You may, or may not, want to probe into the reasons behind the reluctance. Wisdom does not set out to seek all the explanations behind something. Wisdom acknowledges

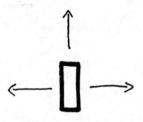

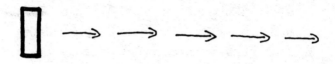

The freedom to move in any direction is only of value if in the end there is a direction in which you wish to move.

the reality of an attitude or value. You do not need to know the explanation for there being a rock in the middle of the road before you acknowledge that fact. When you want to change something you may try to find the reasons behind it.

 # 161 You may drive along the road to get to the beach. You may use the road to get to and from the beach whenever you want.

There does not have to be a choice between the unstructured beach and the structured road. You can make use of the values of both. You can alternate between hedonistic drift and ambitious progression – if that is your design. Many people already do that in their divide between their working lives and their private lives.

Nor does wisdom demand consistency. Consistency is only demanded by self-image and by the expectations of others. Others expect you to be as they know you. You do not always have to oblige them.

 # 162 Wisdom is not just a clever way of deciding between the obvious options. Wisdom is much more concerned with the 'design' of options. There may be ways of combining existing options which seem different. It may be possible to design totally new options. In the choice between working and not working, you may choose to work part-time, or on a temporary basis, or to set up your own business with the possibility of delegating work from time to time.

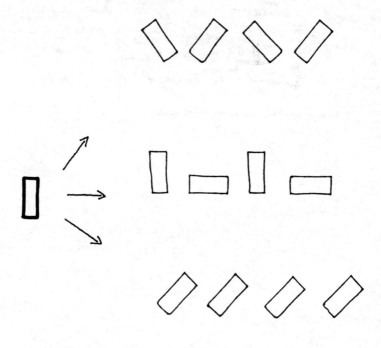

Wisdom is not just choosing between alternatives, but the design of the alternatives themselves.

Whenever alternatives are put before you there is nothing to say that these are the 'only possible' alternatives. You are free to apply your design skills to these alternatives.

That is why 'judgement' is so inadequate as a thinking system. 'Design' is just as important.

 # 163 A tribe of Indians is found in the Amazon. 'Civilization' is getting closer. What do you do? Do you insist that the Indians remain isolated from the larger world, even if this means denying them medicines that would save their sick children? Do you seek to keep them in a cultural cage, like animals in a zoo, for observers to observe? Or do you allow them to find out about the larger world, to try out alcohol, to acquire the outer-world diseases? Do you try to do both by educating some of the Indians but keeping the others in their own community?

Being wise on behalf of others is not easy. Acting moment-to-moment may not be sufficient. There needs to be an overall plan thought out in advance. Maybe there should have been some way of educating some of the Indians on the alternative ways of interacting with the outer world.

 # 164 Perhaps many millions of years ago the dolphins called a great meeting. They considered moving on to land and developing more useful operating limbs. They considered that food was abundant in the sea. The water supported their weight. The temperature of the water was more stable than on land. There were many other advantages mentioned. So they decided to stay in the sea even though they are air-breathing mammals. This may have been a wise choice even if they could not have foreseen the dangers posed by the netting of tuna.

Perhaps the cows in the field have got it right. But then is life, like watching television, time-filling between the events of birth and death?

Wisdom suggests you choose your own answer, and that answer will be right for you at this moment. But not necessarily for ever.

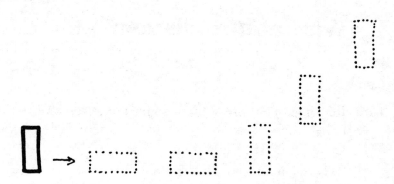

A choice may be right for the moment but does not have to be right for ever.

Wise about Wisdom

 # 165 It is time to be wise about wisdom and to summarize this book.

'Where ignorance is bliss, 'tis folly to be wise.'

This well-known quotation is itself a useful piece of wisdom. The 'wise' in the quotation refers to knowledge. There are times when it is better not to know everything.

The saying could be misinterpreted on the basis that it might indeed be better to be stupid and happy than wise and anxious. The whole point about wisdom is that, used effectively, it reduces your anxiety. The notion of 'stupid and happy' only refers to a very stable world in which nothing ever goes wrong. If you are lucky enough to find such a world then stay there. Otherwise you need wisdom to cope with difficulties.

There is always a concern with confusion. You cannot possibly remember all the points in this book. Many of them you know already. So there is the concern that you will get confused and be worse off than before as you try to 'be wise'. There is also the fear of the paralysis of analysis. You might analyse so much that you never make choices or decisions and never take action. There is the concern that when you first learn to ride a bicycle it is difficult and you can fall off and hurt yourself. So wisdom

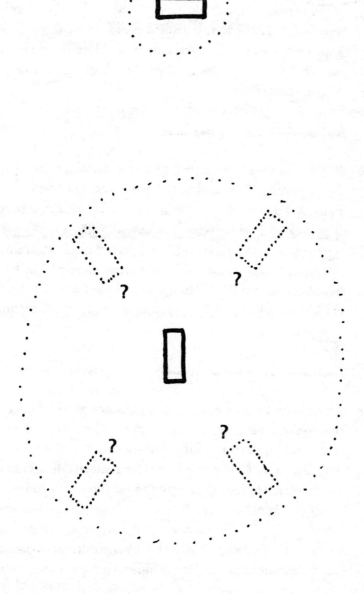

The richer and more complex the world in which you live, the more likely you are to be confused. But it does not have to be so.

may be painful in the beginning. But wisdom is about 'simplifying' life. The bicycle analogy is fine in terms of learning wisdom. You have to make the effort and it may not be easy at first. But the bicycle analogy is not appropriate with regards to falling off. Here we are better off with the 'ice-cream' analogy. You taste it and you like it. You want more.

 # 166　If you develop a gourmet taste for fine food but your finances only allow hamburgers, are you not going to be more disappointed than before you developed that taste? If you do indeed become wise but your life is so dull and uneventful that there is nothing to be 'wise' about, are you not going to be frustrated? Traditionally, wise people have lived very simple lives. Their wisdom has allowed them to choose simplicity. So a simple life does not exclude wisdom.

 # 167　There may be a fear that a consciousness of wisdom will develop into yet another 'conscience'. Like a nagging aunt there will be part of your mind that keeps telling you to 'wise up'. This will be another super-pattern that comes in to advise on choices, decisions and reactions. Do you want a nagging aunt?

Since you are 'designing' this super-pattern you do not have to design it as a 'nagging aunt'.

Far better to think of wisdom as a 'pair of super-spectacles'. When you choose to put them on, the world

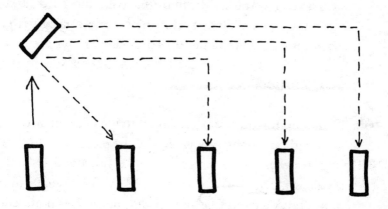

A fear that conscience like a nagging aunt is forever observing, scolding and directing behaviour. . .

becomes much clearer and all the details become more visible. You choose to put on these spectacles whenever you want to. You might find that you have then trained your eyes so well that you can now see clearly without consciously having to put the spectacles on.

 # 168 Read and reread this book. Dip into it whenever you want to. Read only one paragraph. Read a page at night to put you to sleep.

It is a book for grazing, not for devouring. It is not a book you read through in a rush and then say: 'I have read it.'

You are supposed to integrate what you read here with your own experience and wisdom. This integration takes time. You are not standing looking at a picture – you are in the picture.

There is no greater waste of time than to read through this book 'ready to disagree' with as much as possible of what is written. That is just the childish self-indulgence that we too often esteem as criticism.

We need to replace that traditional idiom of the Gang of Three with the analogy of a 'mine'. You work the mine. You get as much out of it as possible. You may have to process what you get out of the mine. It is up to you to find and make value.

That there should be differences of opinion and different perspectives is to be expected. It is part of wisdom to expect plurality. It is not part of wisdom to suppose that,

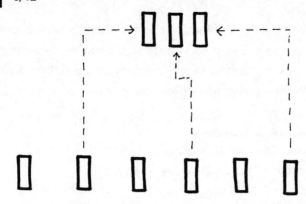

Go through this book picking out the points that make sense to you and putting them together. You can 'graze' through the book as often as you like or dip into it anywhere at any time.

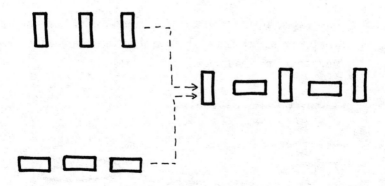

You are supposed to integrate what you read here with your own experience, rather than to choose one or the other. You use what you find to be of value for you.

by definition, your point of view is the only possible one. If by reading this book you define more clearly for yourself your own model of wisdom – which is different from mine – then good luck to you.

 # 169   From time to time in this book there are suggested things 'to do' and also suggested things 'to don't'. There are things to avoid and things to seek out. There are certain traditional habits we have developed which may make wisdom impossible. Just reducing the dominance of such habits is itself the use of wisdom. There are other things, like 'possibility', where we need to develop new habits or encourage the ones we have.

Do you make harsh stereotyping judgements? Perhaps you should be conscious of that habit. Do you make an effort to generate and consider alternatives? Perhaps you should seek to do this more often.

There is no need to list the 'do's' and 'don'ts'. As you read and reread this book the overlays and repetition will make these points for you.

 # 170   Awareness

Wisdom is about awareness. If you know the road, life is easier. If you can see the road, life is easier. If you can discover new roads, life is richer. If you know you have a choice of roads, life is richer.

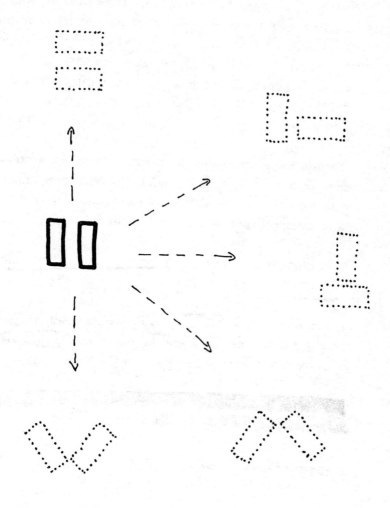

Wisdom is about awareness and possibilities: awareness of the world around; awareness of possibilities and choices.

Awareness can be applied to the outer world. What is going on out there? There may be times when the outer world is going to affect you, either as a threat or as an opportunity. Seeing more clearly what is happening is always an advantage. There are times when you are going to want to affect the outer world. Seeing this world more clearly will enable you to design your actions more effectively.

Awareness can be applied to the inner world. How do we see the world? What are our habits? What am I doing right now? You know what you look like in the mirror. Do you have a mirror for your inner world?

'The purpose of thinking is to arrange the inner and outer world so as to serve and improve our values.'

If you do not know the ingredients, you are not going to be a very good cook. If you do not know the processes of cooking you are not going to be a very good cook.

Awareness is much more than information. Awareness is information as it relates to you.

171 Perception

Perception is not what the 'eye' sees but what the 'brain' sees. When you read the word 'ice-cream' you do not just see an arrangement of letters. In your 'mind's eye' you get an impression of the appearance, taste, texture and temperature of an ice-cream.

When you see a train pulling out of a railway station your perception is very different according to whether it is the train you have just missed or if that train had no relevance for you.

I have often written that we badly need a word in our language for 'the way we look at things'. The nearest word is indeed 'perception' but that is rather too tied up with vision. We need a word to indicate 'the way we see things in our mind'.

Wisdom takes place in perception. Within perception the traditional rules of logic do not apply. We are dealing with the logic of 'flow', or 'water logic', and not the logic of 'identity', or 'rock logic' (see *Water Logic*, Penguin 1994; *I am Right – You are Wrong*, Penguin 1991).

If our perceptions are wrong then no amount of logical excellence will give the right answer. So it is a pity that almost the whole of our traditional intellectual effort has been directed at logic and so little at perception.

Logic will not change emotions and feelings. Perception will.

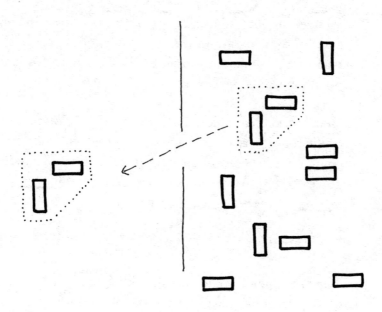

Perception is a matter of picking out the patterns that we have got used to seeing. It becomes difficult to see things in another way unless we make the effort demanded by wisdom.

172 Broad

Cleverness is sharp focus, wisdom is wide angle. Wisdom is largely about 'broadening' perception. Most of the mistakes in thinking are mistakes in perception. Seeing only part of the situation. Jumping to conclusions. Misinterpretation caused by feelings.

Helicopters that report back to local radio stations on traffic conditions at peak hours get a broad view of what is going on. No motorist stuck in the traffic could possibly get this view. With wisdom we seek to climb into a helicopter to get a broad overall view.

There are three types of 'broad'.

The first type of broad is to do with 'width'. How widely do we see? This means taking into account different factors, different people, different values and different needs. This is the closest to the helicopter analogy. We look around in all directions, not just where we are next going to place our feet.

The second type of broad is to do with 'depth'. This means looking forward and looking backwards. We look backwards in time to seek explanations and reasons for what is before us. We look backwards to examine past experiences, both our own and those of other people. We look forward to see the consequences of what is before us. This might be prediction in terms of what may happen. It may also be looking for the consequences of any action we are contemplating. We look forward from the immediate consequences to the long-term consequences.

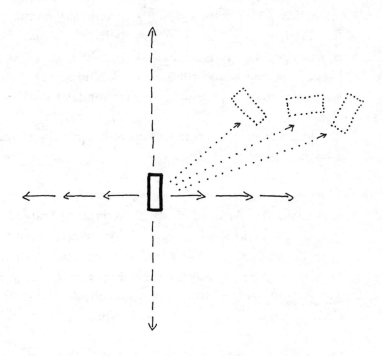

Wisdom is about breadth of perception. There are three types of breadth.

1. How widely do we look? How widely do we see?

2. How deeply do we look? Forward, backwards and into detail.

3. How rich is our vision? This means possibilities, speculations, alternatives and different points of view.

The third type of broad is to do with 'richness'. Here we open up alternatives and different ways of looking at things. We seek out the existing alternatives. We imagine the different viewpoints of other people. We make an effort to generate further alternatives. These are alternatives of perception and alternatives of action. We look for 'might be' and for 'possibly'. We go beyond 'what is'.

So the aim of wisdom is to end up with a perception that is wider, deeper and richer.

There is a considerable element of creativity in broadening perception. We need creativity to direct our attention to areas we might have overlooked. We need creativity to generate alternatives. We need creativity to put things together in different ways. We need creativity to link up with past experiences which are not so obviously relevant. Creative perception is part of perception.

One shoe salesman reported back that there was no market because no one wore shoes. His companion reported back that it was a fantastic market because no one wore shoes.

---

173   Logic Bubble

'Everyone is always right – no one is ever right.'

A logic bubble is that bubble of perceptions and values within which everyone acts logically.

This quote comes from an earlier book (see *Future Positive*, Penguin 1990). What it means is that at any moment everyone is acting logically within his or her 'bubble' of values and perceptions. So at that moment in time that person is 'right'. In the broader, overall and objective sense no one is ever right because we do not have a full understanding of the world or the detailed consequences of our action far into the future.

Wisdom acknowledges the value and the reality of individual logic bubbles.

---

174   Possibly

It must have become obvious to anyone reading this book that 'possibly' and 'possibilities' are a central part of wisdom.

'Possibly' is valuable in two ways.

The first way is 'possibly' in exploration and creativity. Just as the hypothesis is central to science, so our ability to hold something in mind as 'possible' allows us to examine, explore, develop and check out that possibility. Generating 'possible' courses of action allows us to choose between them. Considering 'possible' designs allows us to work towards them. 'Possibly' is a key driver of progress, change and human thinking. It is a pity that traditional thinking seems to have had little time for it, preferring the temptation of certainty.

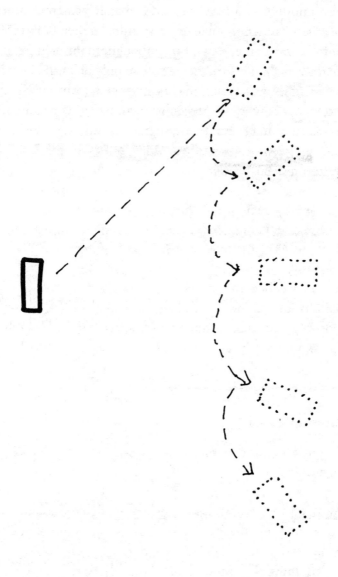

Possibility is the key to wisdom. Possibility is the basis of creativity. Possibility is the best antidote to arrogance. Possibility drives exploration.

The second way that 'possible' is valuable is that it is the best antidote to arrogance and to harsh judgements. Arrogance can assert that there is only one way. 'Possibly' puts forward other ways. Once thought, a thought cannot be unthought. False judgements can only be challenged by 'possibly'. A judgement may be correct in terms of chosen information, chosen perceptions and chosen values. So a logical attack on that judgement will not succeed. But 'possibly' shows other possibilities of information, perception and values.

There may be no proof that improvement can be made in an area. It is only our belief in 'possible' improvement that gets us trying to make that improvement.

Unless we become skilled in 'possibly' we shall always remain far behind the full use of our experience. Only 'possibly' can pull us ahead so that we can put together our experience in different ways.

175 Alternatives

Richness of perception, 'possibly' and alternatives all go together.

We need to seek out and consider available alternatives. These may be alternatives of perception, alternatives of explanation, alternatives of action and alternatives of design. How else can we look at this? How else can we do this?

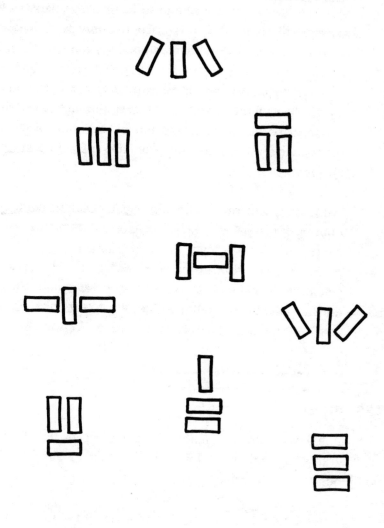

Richness of perception and design are based on alternatives. So is effective action. The design of alternatives is a key element in wisdom.

Without alternatives we remain trapped in one channel. No matter how reasonable a position might be, we need to consider alternatives. Is your view the only possible one? Is this course of action the only possible one?

Alternatives do not have to show themselves. They do not have to 'put up their hands' like a child in a classroom who wants to be noticed. Alternatives do not have to force themselves on your attention. You have to go out and look for them.

Something happens and the immediate response comes to mind. But you pause in order to seek out alternatives.

Sometimes you have to create alternatives. The various deliberate techniques of lateral thinking are available for this purpose. You need to say to yourself: 'Right here I am going to set out to generate some further alternatives.'

176   Plurality

It follows from 'alternatives' that we accept for consideration a number of different possibilities, alternatives, points of view, values, etc.

Traditional thinking says: 'No, you cannot put that on the table unless you can logically justify its being on the table.' There is a judgement gateway. If something does not pass that judgement gateway it is rejected.

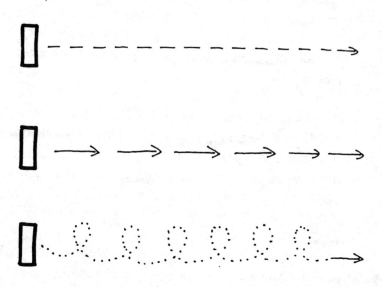

Wisdom encourages different thoughts and different values. This gives a richness of perception. There does not have to be a choice of one and a rejection of the others.

Wisdom says: 'Put it on the table anyway and later we can see whether to use it, combine it with other things or not use it.'

Wisdom encourages plurality in order to get the 'richer' picture.

The Japanese word for yes is '*hai*'. But when a Japanese says '*hai*' it does not mean that he or she is agreeing with you. It simply means that the person is awake and has heard what you have said. That person has 'put it on the table'. Consideration comes later.

---

177   Parallel Thinking

This follows on directly from plurality. Parallel thinking means laying down different views, values and possibilities in parallel.

Parallel thinking is the opposite of traditional adversarial thinking, where each statement has to be judged before being accepted. In adversarial thinking, the 'contradiction' is a very important and powerful tool. Both sides of a contradiction cannot be right. One or other must go. Parallel thinking allows both sides of the contradiction to be laid down in parallel without interfering with each other. Later on, in the design phase, things can be sorted out.

Parallel thinking removes at once the urge to instant judgement. You do not have to accept something as 'right' because you have not rejected it as 'wrong'. You simply accept it 'in parallel'. Sometimes you can accept it as

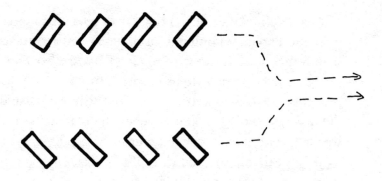

Parallel thinking is the opposite of traditional adversarial thinking. Instead of judgement, both sides are laid down in parallel and then a way forward is designed.

'possibly' but even when you cannot accept something as 'possible' you still accept it in parallel.

Husbands usually complain that wives take far too many clothes on holiday. Husbands say that wives should decide in advance exactly what is going to be needed and to reject what is not going to be needed. Husbands complain that wives take six outfits with them so they can have the 'luxury' of choice at the holiday destination. Parallel thinking is what the wives are doing. They take everything along and then make the choice only when it has to be made. The husbands' thinking is more like traditional Gang of Three thinking: accept or reject at this point before packing it.

---

178   Choice

If you have a map showing the different roads, then you choose the road you want to take according to your needs and values. You may want the shortest route. You may want the route with least traffic. You may want the most scenic route. You may want the road with the best surface. You may want the fastest route (not necessarily the shortest).

It is not the purpose of wisdom to choose your values for you or to change your values. Different readers of this book will have different values. The purpose of wisdom is to allow you to apply your values effectively.

It is possible that over time wisdom may get you to alter your values. Wisdom may suggest that a value you now

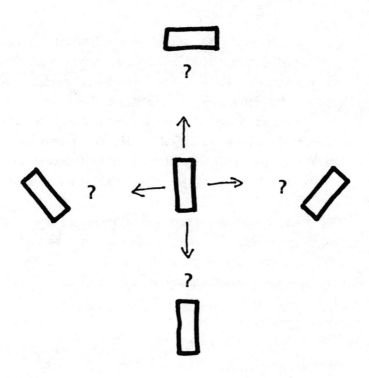

Because wisdom encourages alternatives and possibilities, wisdom also encourages choice according to your values.

hold high is really rather superficial. But changing values is your task.

The important point is that at any moment you are making the choice. If you choose to let someone else or circumstances make the choice for you, that is also your choice. If you prefer to take a step and then let the consequences make a choice for you, that is also your choice. If you choose to follow a leader who is going to make the choices for you, that is also your choice. If you do not want to make a decision – that itself is a decision.

Wisdom accepts that there are times when you do not have a choice or when you only have the illusion of a choice. That is perfectly possible. But wisdom suggests you examine those situations carefully in order to see whether this is really the case or an excuse for inaction.

The 'edge effect' suggests that the first step may be very difficult or very tempting. Wisdom insists that you look forward into the future. If the first step is tempting, wisdom may find the later consequences to be not so attractive. If the first step is difficult, wisdom may find that the later consequences are very beneficial.

The whole purpose of wisdom is to lay out the inner world and outer world in such a way that you can make choices.

179　Values

The purpose of wisdom is to serve your values, the values of your local community and the values of the world. So

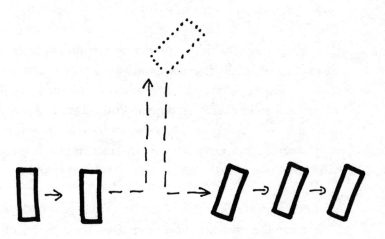

If we determine our values then those values can determine our choices
and behaviour.

values are central. You can explore your values with wisdom. You can develop a 'broad' sense of values in terms of width, depth and richness.

There are the positive values which you seek and the negative values which you seek to avoid.

In any situation there are the values of the actor (usually yourself), of the people directly affected by your action and of those indirectly affected (perhaps through the environment). A broad map of values is what wisdom tries to draw.

There are the obvious values that are easy to remember. Then there is a wide range of less easily noticed values. These are often to do with relationships, position, status, etc. Being given attention and recognition is a high positive value. Boredom is a high negative value.

Not all values are equal. Some have a higher priority than others. Values may need sorting out.

There can be contrary values, either within the same person or between different persons. We can seek to accommodate the contrary values, combine them together or alternate between them. We can 'trade off' values, giving up some in order to enjoy others.

It is the role of the 'design' process to take the values and the broadly perceived situation and to design the way forward. This may be a single design, or the result may be a set of alternatives. You then have to choose between the alternatives, using your values and priorities again.

Design may involve working forward with the key values and then seeking to fit the other values in. Design may involve trying to work forward with all values at the same time.

The elements of design are:

What is desirable?

What is possible?

What are the models?

What are the difficulties?

Is this satisfactory?

180   Emotions and Feelings

Wisdom acknowledges the validity and powerful reality of emotions and feelings. Wisdom attempts to use them for their value and to avoid their negative effects. Overreaction is one obvious negative effect. So is biased perception.

Imagine a square tray suspended by a spring at each corner. In the centre of the level tray there is a motionless ball. A simple channel in the surface runs from the ball to each of the sides. Which of the four channels will the ball follow? You put some weights on the tray in one area. The tray tilts in that direction. The ball rolls down the channel that benefits from the tilt.

In a similar way our feelings and emotions alter the chemical balance in the brain so that certain areas are more sensitized and therefore ready to be activated. Our perception then follows this sensitization or 'biasing'. It is not that we 'choose' to see things in a way that fits our emotions. That is the 'only' way we can perceive at that moment. We therefore need to recognize this biasing property of emotions and make a deliberate effort to bring to the surface some alternative perceptions. They will not just occur by themselves.

Logic is unlikely to change emotions and feelings, but changed perception can.

Emotions and feelings overlap with values but are not always the same thing. Your material value system may tell you that you have done well to sell your house at a large profit. Your feeling may be one of sadness as you move out of the house. You may even feel delighted when

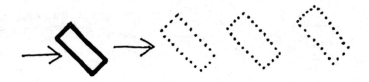

If our emotions come first then they determine our perceptions. We only see things the way we want to see them.

the failure of your business frees you up to do other things that you have always wanted to do.

Awareness of the 'edge effect' may distinguish between temporary feelings and the more valuable long-term ones.

#181 Judgement

We can only move through life because the judgement of 'recognition' tells us at every moment what things are; what things to seek; what things to avoid; what things to use as means to get other things. Without judgement we could not proceed at all.

The danger lies in the harsh, quick and rigid judgements that we require of ourselves and that are required by our traditional thinking habits. Too often we use stereotypes to ease our judgement. Too often we put up false either/or choices to force ourselves, or others, into a certain position. All this is an integral part of the Gang of Three thinking system, with its emphasis on: rejection of the 'untruth'; the search for absolutes; and an inclusion/ exclusion box type of logic with the avoidance of contradiction. This is an excellent system for many purposes but it has its limits and its dangers. In a changing world the 'boxes' derived from the past may no longer be adequate to describe a changed present.

The dangers of judgement lie both in the rejection aspect and in the acceptance aspect. Something rejected drops out of attention and perception. It is no longer an ingredient in our thinking. Something accepted may be

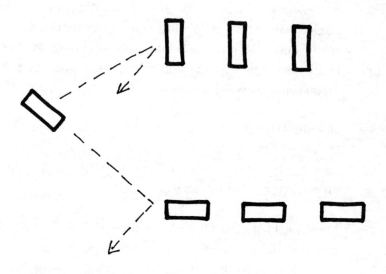

We need judgement to find our way through life. The danger is an excessive emphasis on rigid acceptances and rejections, and not enough attention to design.

accepted too wholeheartedly, when acceptance should be milder, doubtful or related to circumstances. While acknowledging the practicality of simplistic black/white judgements, most people are coming to realize that the world does not work that way. If you choose to take a black and white photograph of the world this does not mean that the world has no colours.

Instead of judgement the emphasis is on 'design'. How do we put things together in order to satisfy our values and needs? Design may be much more difficult than judgement but the results will be better.

Many problems can be solved by analysis. You identify the cause of the problem and then you seek to remove that cause. But when the cause cannot be found or, if found, cannot be removed, then we are paralysed because more and more analysis will not solve that problem. We need to be able to 'design the way forward', leaving the cause in place. While we are excellent at analysis we are not nearly so expert at design – because design requires creativity.

182 Design

How do you design a meal? How do you design a dish? People are designing things every day. Design is not something which only architects and dress designers do. There are times when design may be complicated and difficult but most of the time it is relatively easy. How do you put things together to achieve what you want?

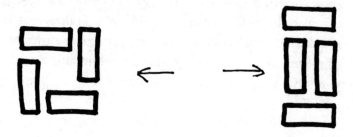

Design is a matter of putting things together to achieve an objective and to serve our values. Instead of searching for the standard solution we design a way forward.

.

It is true that in traditional thinking you may seek to put together the 'thesis' and 'anti-thesis' in the process of 'synthesis'. This means that you seek to combine opposing views. But this is only one small aspect of design. There may be alternatives which are not present in either point of view. There are times when the combining of opposing views is enough, but in general design is a much broader process.

With wisdom we seek to design the way forward rather than 'judge' the way forward.

What is the purpose of design? To satisfy our own and other people's values, in a practical way.

Traditional education systems put far too little emphasis on design. There is a belief that the 'lawyer-type' search for the truth of the Gang of Three is sufficient. Arguments around this matter make use of exactly those habits which the argument is trying to change. It is like speaking French to teach the French to speak English.

Design is the necessary final stage of parallel thinking. We lay things down in parallel in order to provide the ingredients for design. Sometimes the outcome is obvious and reveals itself. At other times a more deliberate design process is required.

Does this mean that design is always better than judgement? Not at all. That would be contrary to the spirit of wisdom. There are times when judgement is required. There are times when judgement is faster and better than design. There are times when judgement is needed even within the design process. In the end judgement is required to assess and choose the outputs from design. We come back to the 'salt curve'. No judgement is bad. Some judgement is good. Excessive judgement is bad. What do we mean by 'excessive'? The belief that judgement is sufficient by itself. It is only that arrogance which needs challenging.

Just as we need a better word for 'perception', we also need a better word for 'design'. The word 'design' has strong connections to interior design, graphic design, dress design, etc. All these suggest visual appearance and, perhaps, something added on to the essentials. In its broadest sense design means 'putting things together to serve our values'.

Consider two architects. The first architect sits in his office with a great folder of standard designs. The client goes in and explains his or her needs. The architect pauses. Then, like the doctor diagnosing measles, the architect says: 'It is design number 71 that you will be wanting.' So the architect opens the file at page 71 and shows the client what he or she will be getting.

The other architect listens carefully to what the client wants in terms of living space, use, access, working environment, storage, cost and appearance, and then asks the client to come back at a later date. The architect then sets out to design a house. It is true that this design may resemble other designs. It is true that the designed house may contain sub-elements that are standard. Nevertheless, there is a design effort.

We have got far too used to considering only the 'doctor model' of the first architect, who seeks to recognize standard patterns, instead of considering the 'architect model' of the second architect. The reason we have done this is that the historic tradition of thinking in the Western world was concerned with 'discovering the truth' (as required in theology) rather than in 'designing for value'.

One of the difficulties of design is that we feel compelled to 'design for perfection'. How can we get this absolutely right? This makes design very much harder than judgement. As a general policy it is best to aim for a 'simple and practical' design. Then you seek to improve this design. If you cannot improve the design then use it as it is.

Knowing that a 'judgement' is right is almost an emotion. The brain is set up to make judgements. When we recognize something, the processes in the brain provide a sort of 'click', just as humour generates a laugh. Occasionally this happens with design. At other times our emotions start to come into play. We get to like the design. We like it more and more. At other times we are left to make the practical choice between designs, none of which inspire us.

Not all meals have to be memorable experiences. Most meals are designs for a practical purpose. They achieve that purpose. This does not exclude excellence but it does not demand excellence on every occasion.

 # 183   If you find wisdom a 'plus', then use it. If you believe that you are sufficiently wise already then congratulations either on your excellence or on your self-deception.

Wisdom is not instead of logic. Wisdom is the operating system of 'perception'. Logic only begins when perception ends.

How are you going to put wisdom into practice? You can read this book and reread it. You can integrate some of the thoughts and suggestions into your own habits of thought. What is put forward here is based on more than twenty-five years' direct involvement in the teaching of thinking to schoolchildren, adults and the senior executives of some of the world's largest corporations (employing up to 400,000 people).

As a practical step you may even wish to design for yourself a new super-pattern. Just as King Arthur of the Round Table was always rushing off to the wizard Merlin for wisdom, so you can create your own Merlin. What would Merlin do here? What would the 'wise person' do here?

You would then use this super-pattern as you wished, just as you use the gears as you wish when driving a car. Perhaps, in time, you will progress from a manual gear-shift car to an automatic one. Wisdom will now become part of your behaviour.

If you find that wisdom has no value for you, give this book to someone who needs it as much as you do.

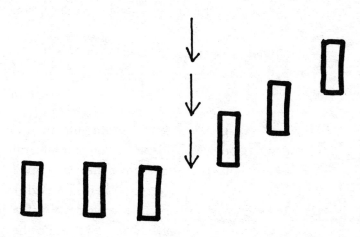

Wisdom comes with growth. But wisdom is also the fertilizer for growth.